D. J. Wintridge

A Handbook for
PRIMARY MATHEMATICS CO-ORDINATORS

This book was written by members of the Mathematics Education Section of the National Association of Teachers in Further and Higher Education. A list of the contributors can be found on page ix.

The preparation of this text was supported by the Mathematical Education Trust. The Trust was established to support work in mathematical education directly useful in schools, and the preparation of texts for practising teachers and others concerned with mathematics in the classroom.

A Handbook for
PRIMARY
MATHEMATICS
CO-ORDINATORS

Edited by
DAVID J. WINTERIDGE

P·C·P
Paul Chapman
Publishing Ltd

This edition first published 1989
Paul Chapman Publishing Ltd
144 Liverpool Road
London
N1 1LA

British Library Cataloguing in Publication Data
Winteridge, D. J.
   Handbook for primary mathematics co-ordinators.
   1. Primary schools. Curriculum subjects: Mathematics.
   Teaching
   I. Title
   372.7′3044

ISBN 1 85396 054 3

Typeset by Burns & Smith, Derby
Printed by St Edmundsbury Press, Bury St Edmunds
Bound by W. H. Ware & Sons Ltd, Clevedon.

CONTENTS

CONTRIBUTORS

The main contributors are all members of the National Association of Teachers in Further Education, Mathematics Education Section.

David ('Bud') Winteridge is Principal Lecturer and Head of Mathematics at Newman and Westhill Colleges in Birmingham. He is director of a number of in-service courses for teachers including one for primary mathematics co-ordinators.

Melvyn Brown is Senior Lecturer in Mathematics Education at Newcastle upon Tyne Polytechnic, having had experience in primary and middle schools and the advisory service. He has designed and taught several courses for mathematics co-ordinators in primary and middle schools.

John Costello is Lecturer in Education at Loughborough University, with responsibility for courses concerned with teaching mathematics.

Rita Crust is currently a research assistant at the Shell Centre for Mathematical Education, University of Nottingham. While at Matlock College of Higher Education she was director of a variety of in-service courses, including diploma courses for primary mathematics co-ordinators.

Marion Dunkerley is Head of the Mathematics Section at North Cheshire College and Director of the joint Cheshire County/College Mathematics Unit, from which the Cheshire Mathematics Support Team provides in-service and the ESG initiative in schools throughout the county.

Lindy Furby taught in primary schools in the ILEA for 14 years. She has been a Primary Mathematics Consultant and now works as a Senior Lecturer in Mathematics Education at Bradford and Ilkley Community College.

Gwen Renton is now retired after teaching for nearly twenty years at the College of Ripon and York St. John. She is still active in education as a governor of her local village school.

Angela Walsh is Deputy-Director of the National Curriculum Council PrIME project. She has been involved in in-service training for primary teachers for many years including directing a diploma course for mathematics co-ordinators. Her teaching experience spans both primary and secondary phases.

Other contributors were:

Tricia Barthorpe, Head of Special Needs, Vale of Ancholme Secondary School, Brigg, South Humberside.

Daphne Kerslake, Principal Lecturer in Mathematics Education, Bristol Polytechnic.

Derek Woodrow, Head of Educational Studies, Didsbury School of Education, Manchester Polytechnic.

PREFACE

During the past 30 years there have been considerable changes in primary school mathematics. In the 1960s a number of publications, initiated by such organizations as the Mathematical Association, the Schools Council and the Nuffield Foundation, advocated a new approach to primary mathematics. The view put forward was that children would best learn mathematics through actively responding to practical experiences, coupled with discussion and guided discovery. Moreover, the changes advocated were not only in approach but also in content. The syllabus was enlarged to include a variety of mathematical topics related to shape, mensuration, pictorial representation, probability and logic in addition to the traditional diet of arithmetic. These ideas were brought to the attention of teachers through the work of Miss Biggs and the Nuffield Project.

After the publication of the Nuffield Guides, the next 15 years or so saw the publication of a considerable number of children's textbook schemes. These schemes rapidly became more comprehensive. In addition to textbooks, the published schemes were supplemented by a variety of other materials for pupils, including workcards, worksheets and, later, computer software. Most importantly, the schemes included very detailed, comprehensive teachers' handbooks. So 'Fletcher', 'Scottish', 'Nuffield', 'Peak', 'Ginn', and so on, became the basis of much mathematics teaching in primary and middle schools.

From the late 1970s to the present day a number of very influential reports have appeared. These have come from such groups as Her Majesty's Inspectorate (HMI), the Assessment of Performance Unit (APU), the Cockcroft Committee and, more recently, the National Curriculum Council

(NCC). Several of these reports have commented on the effectiveness of the changes in primary mathematics. A number of them stress the importance of having someone nominated to take responsibility for curriculum leadership in mathematics. Such people, at one time known as post-holders for mathematics, rapidly became known as mathematics co-ordinators, after the phrase was used in the Cockcroft Report (1982).

A recent survey by Marion Stow (1988), on behalf of the NFER, showed that in a sample of 1,507 primary and middle schools about 45 per cent had a teacher (as distinct from Headteacher or Deputy Head) mathematics co-ordinator. Of the remaining schools, in nearly 19 per cent the post was given to the Deputy Head and in the remaining 36 per cent the responsibility for mathematics rested with the Headteacher. These figures, however, are somewhat distorted by the situation in small schools where the very small number of staff or the lack of incentive allowances makes it impossible to appoint anyone other than the Head or Deputy as mathematics co-ordinator. For schools with 150 pupils or more, just over 60 per cent have someone other than the Head or Deputy as co-ordinator. The salary structure of main professional scale plus incentive allowances, make it likely that such posts have increased since the structure was introduced in 1987.

Marion Stow's report also suggests that, although those in post considered they were effective in carrying out their roles in relation to implementing a scheme of work and to organizing and maintaining resources, they were less sure about their effectiveness in such matters as assessing children's work, monitoring mathematics work throughout the school, liaising with other schools and identifying special educational needs in mathematics. Also, 33 per cent 'indicated great need for in-service education' and only 7 per cent of co-ordinators 'indicated that they had little need for in-service education'.

This book has been written to help mathematics co-ordinators clarify their role, cope with the many demands of the post and develop the professional skills necessary to do the job effectively. It can be read, or dipped into, by an individual teacher or it could be used to supplement an in-service course.

Initial training courses now include some preparation for a specialist curriculum leadership role and this book provides suitable reading for that aspect of BEd and PGCE courses.

A current major item of concern for mathematics co-ordinators is the implementation of the National Curriculum. At the time this book was being written the proposals for the mathematics component of the National Curriculum were just being released. This book attempts to give due attention to these proposals, as they stand at the time of publication.

References

Cockcroft, W. H. (Chairman) (1982) *Mathematics Counts* (Report of the Committee of Inquiry), HMSO, London.

Stow, M. with Foxman, D. (1988) *Mathematics Co-ordination*, NFER-Nelson, Windsor.

Editor's Note   Throughout this book the phrase 'primary school' has been used to signify any school where primary-age pupils are taught, and hence encompasses infant, junior, first, middle and preparatory schools.

ACKNOWLEDGEMENTS

The editor wishes to express his thanks to the two typists responsible for preparing the final draft of the book, Mrs Annette Winteridge and Mrs Mary Green, for their accurate and prompt work.

The editor and publishers wish to thank the following for permission to use copyright material:

HMSO for extracts from *Mathematics Counts* and *Mathematics from 5-16: Curriculum Matters 3*. Reproduced with the permission of the Controller of HMSO.

SCDC Publications/Longman for the material on page 29 and page 78, from Shuard, H. (1986) *Primary Mathematics Today and Tomorrow*.

Open University/Croom Helm for the material on page 156 from Easen, P. (1985) *Making School-Centred INSET Work*.

NARE for the extract on page 152 from Turnbull, J. (1981, 1987, 1989) *Maths Links*, Volumes 1 and 2, obtainable from NARE, 2 Lichfield Road, Stafford ST17 47X.

ILEA for the extract on page 153 from *Checkpoints* Assessments Cards (1980), ILEA Learning Resources Branch.

ACKNOWLEDGMENTS

1
THE ROLE OF THE
CO-ORDINATOR: AN OVERVIEW

Introduction

For many years primary teachers with a special interest in mathematics have acted as a focus for developing the mathematics curriculum in their schools and for giving support to colleagues who sought their assistance. Recently the title of mathematics co-ordinator has been introduced into school, and recognized as a post of special responsibility. The document *Mathematics Counts* (the Cockcroft Report, 1982) strongly advocates the appointment of a mathematics co-ordinator in a primary school and defines the role in terms of a list of duties. Using this list as a framework each item will be discussed in greater detail to form a more comprehensive picture of the overall role of the co-ordinator. Many of the points raised here are considered in more detail in later chapters.

What then are the duties of the mathematics co-ordinator in a primary school? The Cockcroft Report lists them as follows:

In our view it should be part of the duties of the mathematics co-ordinator to:
- prepare a scheme of work for the school in consultation with the head teacher and staff and, where possible, with schools from which the children come and to which they go (we discuss this further in paragraph 363);
- provide guidance and support to other members of staff in implementing the scheme of work, both by means of meetings and by working alongside individual teachers;
- organize and be responsible for procuring, within the funds made available, the necessary teaching resources for mathematics, maintain an up-to-date inventory and ensure that members of staff are aware of how to use the

resources which are available;

- monitor work in mathematics throughout the school, including methods of assessment and record-keeping;
- assist with the diagnosis of children's learning difficulties and with their remediation;
- arrange school-based in-service training for members of staff as appropriate;
- maintain liaison with schools from which children come and to which they go, and also with LEA advisory staff.

(Cockcroft, 1982, paragraph 355)

Background information about the Cockcroft Report and other documents referred to in this chapter can be found on page 9.

The introduction of the National Curriculum with its related assessment and testing procedures is unlikely to alter the fundamental responsibilities of the mathematics co-ordinator. It may mean, however, that certain areas of responsibility receive, at least in the short term, extra emphasis. *The National Curriculum 5–16: A Consultation Document* (DES, 1987b) makes it clear that it is for schools to decide how the curriculum is to be organized and taught. The *Task Group on Assessment and Testing Report* 'recognizes that the assessments of individual children must continue to be the responsibility of teachers, and that teachers' assessments should be used as a fundamental part of the system' (DES, 1988b, p.6).

The two aspects, organizing the mathematics curriculum and devising methods of assessment, have always been central to the work of the mathematics co-ordinator. The coming of the National Curriculum will ensure that this remains the case, albeit within a framework of statutory arrangements, and these two aspects must be the cornerstones of the school's policy for mathematics teaching.

First and foremost it must be emphasized that any policy must be developed as a collaborative exercise. You, as a co-ordinator, must take responsibility for initiating a policy for mathematics teaching in your school but any hopes you may have of bringing about a real change in existing practices will be doomed unless you have the involvement, the agreement and the co-operation of your colleagues. In Chapter 12 we look in more detail about how policies can be formulated and how changes can be implemented.

The support of the headteacher

Clearly the support of the headteacher is crucial if the co-ordinator is to function effectively. As the co-ordinator, you will need to discuss with the head exactly how you see your role and the sort of support you require. You will also need to clarify how the head sees you fitting into the overall pattern of the school. From the head comes the authority to initiate development, especially in the early stages of establishing a co-ordinator in school. The head can provide the right atmosphere, forging links between you and the staff, the parents, the local education authority (LEA) and other bodies with whom you may not yet be familiar. If the head is seen to encourage you in the early stages and is prepared to explain your role and emphasize his/her support to the rest of the staff, then you have the first essential of a sound basis upon which to develop. Without a good working relationship between you and the headteacher the value of a co-ordinator is greatly diminished.

Modification of your timetable

To be an effective co-ordinator you will need time to work outside your own classroom alongside other teachers, liaise with other schools and, most importantly, to be involved in in-service training for your own development. It is essential that the headteacher recognizes these needs and provides a suitably modified timetable. In the Cockcroft Report this is discussed in some detail in paragraph 723 where it is emphasized that, despite the difficulties of arranging modified timetables, time must be made available for the co-ordinator to carry out his/her role effectively[1]. If necessary, part-time staff should be used to provide cover to free the co-ordinator.

In-service training of the co-ordinator

To supply the necessary stimuli so that staff are aware of new developments and willing to participate in the continued development of the mathematics curriculum the co-ordinator needs in-service support to keep abreast of recent developments and have the opportunity to discuss the role with other co-ordinators and in-service leaders. Your role is to inspire confidence and provide support and guidance within your school. This is a continuing process and to be effective you need regular access to appropriate in-service training yourself.

A very good way of receiving in-service training is by working alongside other teachers. Workshops and group sessions relevant to the work of primary mathematics co-ordinators are often organized by professional associations, by LEAs or by institutions. These are sometimes arranged for weekends or evenings or may require day release. Your local mathematics adviser should be able to give you information on these – and help you to obtain day release if required! Try to enrol on a course where there will be plenty of opportunity to discuss and to exchange ideas, and to work with other mathematics co-ordinators on problems of common interest.

Schemes of work

A major responsibility of your role may be the preparation of a scheme of work. The introduction of a new scheme of work into a school or the revision of the current scheme can often be a traumatic experience and if everybody does not feel fully involved in the change then it is difficult to implement. A scheme of work can only provide a framework and it is the acceptance and involvement not only of the school but also of the parents that ensures its success.

The *National Curriculum, Mathematics for Ages 5 to 16* (DES, 1988d) has clearly indicated 'programmes of study'. The programmes are defined in terms of 'levels of attainment'. Levels 1–3 specify the programmes of study for pupils aged 5–7 years and levels 2–6 specify the programmes of study for pupils aged 7–11 years. There is a danger that these programmes will be seen as all that is required by way of a scheme of work, but this should not be the case. A scheme of work should pay attention to the objectives of mathematics teaching, the mathematical processes to be encountered, the resources to be used and the teaching methods to be adopted. The National Curriculum provides a necessary framework but each school (and each teacher) will have to put their own 'flesh on the bare bones'[2].

Chapter 3 of *Curriculum Matters 3* (DES, 1987a) considers the criteria that might determine the content of the mathematics curriculum. It provides ten criteria against which 'decisions about mathematical content in relation to the differing needs of all pupils from 5 to 16 should be governed'. As a reminder it is worth listing these here:

1. Mathematical content needs to be chosen so that the pupils for whom it is intended can cover it successfully at their own appropriate level.
2. Mathematical content should not be so extensive that it imposes restrictions on the range of classroom approaches.
3. Mathematical content should form a coherent structure.
4. Mathematical content should be sufficiently broad for all pupils.
5. Mathematical content should meet the mathematical needs of the rest of the curriculum.
6. Mathematical content should meet the basic mathematical needs of adult life, including employment.
7. Mathematical content should include elements that are intrinsically interesting and important.
8. In choosing mathematical content appropriate weighting should be given to key aspects.
9. Mathematical content should take account of the potential of electronic calculators.

10. The content should be influenced increasingly by developments in microcomputing.

Discussion of this chapter with colleagues can provide a useful focus in preparing a scheme of work. Likewise in Chapters 4 and 5 of the same document (DES, 1987a), classroom approaches and assessment are discussed and again their implications are essential in developing a scheme of work. In Chapter 8 of this book we discuss schemes of work in some detail.

Guidance and support to other members of staff

It is essential that staff understand and feel at ease with the *approach* to mathematics teaching as well as its organization. Many primary school teachers lack confidence in their own mathematical abilities and the presence of a co-ordinator can appear threatening. So the right atmosphere must be fostered in which staff can develop confidence and a willingness to discuss mathematics both with you and amongst themselves.

The role of the co-ordinator in providing the right sort of support, not only with individual teachers but with and between groups of teachers, is very important. This area obviously links with the provision of school-based in-service training.

In-service training of colleagues

Another responsibility of the co-ordinator is arranging school-based in-service training. This is a vital role. If the school is to develop mathematically everybody must be involved. By the nature of the teaching profession teachers can become isolated in their classrooms. The role of the co-ordinator is to ensure that the in-service training provided equips the teacher to develop the curriculum in the classroom. This requires providing teachers with the necessary skills to identify and meet the needs of their children. Giving colleagues the opportunity to come into your classroom and watch and share in your teaching can create an open atmosphere that will encourage other staff to do the same.

As you monitor the mathematics throughout the school you should note specific contributions that individual staff can make to, and particular areas that would benefit from, some in-service work, such as certain aspects of the mathematics scheme you are using. Of course, the preparation of the scheme as discussed above would be an important feature of in-service work. Contributions to your programme could involve the use of colleagues with whom you have made contact outside school.

Resources

It is useful to prepare a list of the apparatus and resources available in your school and to examine it in the light of the aims, objectives, content and classroom approach of your curriculum.

Ensuring that staff are aware of how to use available resources should become part of your school-based in-service role. Given the financial constraints of schools it is well worthwhile considering if the resources already present in school can be used more widely. Many very successful courses have been based on the examination of a resource that has been tucked away or relegated to a particular age group. The use of structured logic material only in the infant school is an example of this. Yet it has applications at all age levels of mathematical ability.

In Chapter 12 of the Cockcroft Report (1982) there is a discussion of the facilities that should be available in schools. Also the HMI Report *A Handbook of Suggestions* (DES, 1979) lists resources needed to develop a topic across the primary school.

Monitoring work in mathematics throughout the school

The essential role of the co-ordinator to monitor work in mathematics throughout the school brings us back to the importance of the headteacher's support. To be effective you will need the time to work alongside individual teachers so that you can develop a complete picture of what is happening at each stage. Hence a suitable timetable is necessary. For many teachers, working with another teacher in their classroom may be a new experience and possibly one which, at first, is not altogether welcome. So it is important that you discuss in detail how you intend to work together and establish a good relationship. The role of monitoring should give you a clear view of how to continue the development of the mathematics curriculum.

Since you will have a more complete picture of the whole school's mathematics than other teachers you may, when working alongside a colleague, diagnose a difficulty that possibly has its cause earlier in the school. By discussion on an individual basis or within a group you can consider the nature of the children's learning difficulties, and their remedy. Then you can monitor how effectively these problems are overcome. Most learning difficulties will be well known to the class teacher, and as part of your role of guidance and support you should be willing to listen to the class teacher so that both of you are fully involved in the diagnosis and remedy of these difficulties. The individual topic chapters in *A Handbook of Suggestions* (DES, 1979) provide detailed descriptions of the stages of development which can help in both of these areas.

It is important that other members of staff are kept abreast of new trends and developments in mathematics education and are fully involved in planning and implementing changes to mathematics teaching in their school. Assessment and testing will play an important part in the implementation of the National Curriculum. The Task Group on Assessment and Testing (TGAT) reported in 1988 and proposed that assessment should be by a combination of national standardized tests or 'Standard assessment tasks' (SATS) and teachers' own assessments (TA). The SATS will be applied nationally from a bank of items and, as co-ordinator for mathematics, you will need to be conversant with the types of extended, long and short tasks that your pupils will be confronted with at the ages of 7 and 11 years. Helping to acquaint your colleagues with the types of items will also be seen as part of your duties.

Assessment by teachers (TA) may take a variety of forms and it may be that your LEA adopts, or recommends, a common procedure for its primary schools. However, any procedures will evolve and develop as experience suggests changes and modifications. You should ensure that you represent the opinions of your colleagues in any discussions with groups of teachers and that, within your school, the procedures are understood and agreed with colleagues.

Methods of assessment must be compatible with the mathematics scheme and should reflect the teaching approach used by the school. The increased emphasis on problem-solving and investigational work has meant that personal qualities such as perseverance, creativity, confidence and originality need to be considered when assessing a pupil's performance in mathematics.

Clearly assessment and record-keeping will be a major area of concern for you and you will need to seek help and advice from outside agenices. It will, no doubt, also be the focus of much school-based in-service work.

Liaison with other schools

Establishing and maintaining liaison with schools from which your children come and to which they go is vital if pupils' mathematical education is to be cohesive throughout their school career. You may find that very little liaison has been established and that you will need to establish or re-establish links. The advisory staff can help but often you will need to make the effort to contact these schools yourself. For many children transfer from infant to junior/middle and especially junior/middle to secondary causes uncertainty. Mathematics schemes, styles of teaching, organization etc. can all change dramatically. The greater the co-operation and understanding of teachers across the whole of the educational system the more mathematics teaching will benefit. In some primary schools during their last term children attend special lessons in the secondary school with both their primary and secondary teachers working in co-operation. More frequently secondary school teachers visit the feeder primary schools and talk to the children. What *is* important is that teachers should understand what is happening at each stage of the child's school career. The Cockcroft Report (1982) discusses the problems of continuity on transfer in Chapter 8. Much of the dissatisfaction that occurs over the transfer of children from one school to another is due to lack of communication and understanding between staff in the different areas. Often teachers in primary schools feel reluctant to discuss mathematics with secondary school mathematics specialists. Yet once a rapport is established the secondary teachers are frequently surprised about the range and depth of the work that can be achieved in the primary school. It is often not reflected in the various profiles that accompany the child at transfer, so establishing good relationships between staff is essential for the child's continuing mathematical education.

Working with teachers from the secondary school on a joint project is a good way of improving relationships, of getting to know each other, and of learning about both the content and the style of each other's mathematics teaching. Jointly organizing a display of children's work focused on a particular theme is one way of getting the schools to work together. Alternatively the schools might collaborate to devise a Maths Trail, for different ages and abilities, using the local environment, or they might co-operate on some problem-solving projects. It may require tact and some initiative from you but will be well worth it in the end.

A simple, but very effective way of promoting liaison, used by some groups of schools, is to interchange members of staff for a few lessons. Primary teachers visit the secondary school to carry out some simple investigational or project work with the first year secondary pupils while the secondary teachers teach the top junior pupils. The advantage of this system is that the amount of interchange can be as much or as little as required within the obvious logistical constraints. However, it does require a spirit of co-operation and a preparedness to approach the new situation with confidence but with an open mind.

Another increasingly important area is working with parents. The levels achieved in the various profile components at ages 7 and 11 must be conveyed to the parents together with what proportion of children, both within the school and nationally, reached the various levels. This will provide only the basic information and, as ever, it will be necessary not only to explain the system and discuss the pupil's individual strengths and weaknesses with the parents but also to indicate something of the aims of the mathematics curriculum. As co-ordinator much of the responsibility for this is likely to be yours. This is discussed further in Chapter 8.

Other considerations

There are many other points we could add to the list. The place of mathematics across the whole primary curriculum is most important and part of your role should be to provide the link. This will involve co-operation with co-ordinators or teachers with special responsibilities for other curriculum areas.

You will probably be asked to take some initiative for mathematical displays. While displays should have impact and be changed frequently, they should not become over-burdensome and impede good teaching. A small display can be most effective. The Cockcroft Report (1982) discusses the display of materials and pupils' work in paragraph 614, and a detailed discussion is given in Chapter 7 of this book.

Finally, and most importantly, you will need to consider how to evaluate the quality of mathematics teaching that is taking place. On a simple level you might refer to some of the results obtained from tests but the real quality will be evident in the enthusiasm of both staff and pupils to involve themselves with mathematics in its broadest contexts. When staff and pupils are willing to tackle problems and investigate with confidence, and learn from self-correction, then we are seeing quality in mathematics education. The true quality of mathematics teaching may be at its highest when the child uses the teacher as a support to his/her learning rather than a director of it.

To achieve quality in mathematics teaching you will, as a co-ordinator, need to use all the resources, both human and material, that you have available. As you will be well aware it is not a simple task but it is a highly rewarding one.

Background information

Several publications have been referred to in this chapter and these are listed in the references at the end. You will find it helpful to have access to these and we briefly describe them here.

Mathematics Counts (the Cockcroft Report)

Published in 1982, this was the report of a committee of inquiry into the teaching of mathematics in schools. It is a wide-ranging document, reporting, commenting and making suggestions on many areas of mathematics education and its relation to adult life, employment, schools and in-service training. In it there are three major references to the role of the co-ordinator.

The first of these occurs in paragraphs 354 and 358 in the chapter on mathematics in the primary years. The report states the need for a co-ordinator, gives a list of what in the committee's view should be part of the duties of the mathematics co-ordinator and discusses the support the co-ordinator will require from the headteacher. It also suggests that the responsibility of the post warrants additional salary increments.

The second main reference occurs in the chapter on in-service support for teachers of mathematics, paragraphs 721 to 723. Paragraph 721 expands on the discussion in paragraph 357 and the support needed from the headteacher. Paragraphs 722 and 723 make suggestions for school-based in-service activities and consider the important matters of support and training for the co-ordinator.

The third reference, in paragraphs 772 to 773, considers the role of the co-ordinator in the middle school and whilst this is not strictly within the scope of our discussion the section makes similar points to those considered in the earlier paragraphs.

Mathematics 5–11: A Handbook of Suggestions

This is quite a different document from the Cockcroft Report (1982). It was published in 1979 following the National Survey of Primary Education carried out by HM Inspectorate between 1975 and 1977. This survey provided examples of good practice in primary school mathematics and provided a basis for the *Handbook* to 'identify those parts of the subject which, in HMI's view, should be taught to every child and gives some guidance on approaches which teachers have found to be effective'.

As the title states this is a handbook of suggestions and it contains chapters on specific topics taught in the primary school, communication, language and logic, number, measurement, pictorial and graphical representation, and shape. Each chapter deals with the development of the topic across the primary school and directs the teaching of it. In the preface and introduction there is some valuable background information about the teaching of mathematics, while Chapter 2 looks at the place of mathematics in the primary school, and Chapter 3 considers the planning of the mathematics programme. At the end of the book there are two appendices: the first deals with what in HMI's view should be the main objectives for a majority of children aged 11 years; and the second with types of structural apparatus in common use.

The role of the co-ordinator is not explicitly discussed nor is the term used. The book is addressed to, amongst others, teachers with special responsibilities for mathematics, and in Chapter 3 is a section on teacher development which suggests that support to the classroom teacher is best achieved in those schools that have one teacher with special knowledge of and interest in mathematics, who has some responsibility to undertake the in-service education of other members of staff.

Mathematics from 5 to 16: Curriculum Matters 3

Published in 1985, this is an HMI publication like *A Handbook of Suggestions*. It forms part of a discussion series which includes *English from 5 to 16* and *The Curriculum from 5 to 16*. A major strength of *Curriculum Matters 3* is that it builds on the Cockcroft Report and *A Handbook of Suggestions*, developing many topics discussed in them. In *Curriculum Matters 3* attention is focused on the aims and objectives for teaching mathematics and it considers their implications for the choice of content, the approaches to be used and the assessment of pupils' progress.

By the very nature of the document no direct reference is made to the role of the co-ordinator, but the content discusses the development of the mathematics curriculum in a way that reflects directly on your role. Overall this document brings together and develops both the previous documents and examines certain aspects in greater detail, for instance personal qualities, positive attitudes and the relationship between assessment and classroom approaches.

National Curriculum documents

There are several documents about the National Curriculum which are of particular importance to a mathematics co-ordinator. The initial document *A Consultation Document* ('The Red Book') described the framework for a national curriculum. Publications by the Task Group on Assessment and Testing (TGAT) provide more information, but not subject-specific, about the administration and organization of a national scheme of testing. *TGAT: A Report* was published in 1988 and a booklet, *TGAT: A Digest for Schools* ('The Small Green Book') was made available to all schools by mid-1988.

Of special interest to mathematics co-ordinators will be the two reports of the National Curriculum Mathematics Working Group. The first of these, *Interim Report* ('The Blue Book') is fairly brief but provides a background to the Group's thoughts about the nature and scope of mathematics, how mathematical learning takes place and the implications of this for pupils' attitudes and their personal qualities. The main report, *Mathematics for Ages 5 to 16*, was published in August 1988 and contains the Group's recommendations on attainment targets, profile components and programmes of study. Following consultation on the proposals contained within this document, the National Curriculum Council (NCC) produced the Mathematics Consultation Report in December 1988. The NCC's proposals for attainment targets and programmes of study provided the basis for the statutory orders, which were published in a ring-binder as *Mathematics in the National Curriculum*, by the DES and Welsh Office in April 1989.

Summary

To conclude this chapter you may find it useful to review again some of the main issues that a mathematics co-ordinator has to consider. These are expressed in terms of questions.

1. Have you a clearly defined job description?
2. Whether or not this is the case, how do *you* see your role?
3. Have you discussed your role with the headteacher? With your colleagues?
4. How can you evaluate and monitor the effectiveness of the mathematics teaching in your school?
5. Are the needs of the children being met in mathematics?
6. What do you consider to be the priorities – content, assessment and recording, resources?
7. How can you ensure that you and your colleagues work collaboratively?
8. How can you provide the appropriate support and guidance for colleagues?
9. What in-service activities could you organize?

The list is endless and the task will seem daunting, but giving even tentative answers to these questions will help you to identify your priorities and hence make a start on what can be both a very demanding and a very rewarding job.

Notes

1. A recent HMI report (1989) suggests that although the number of schools with a mathematics co-ordinator has increased, only in a relatively few schools did the co-ordinator have time to carry out all the duties of the post effectively.

2. The non-statutory guidance of the National Curriculum Council (DES, 1989) suggests ways in which a school policy statement, describing the purposes, nature and management of the mathematics taught and learned in the school, can be formulated.

References

Cockcroft, W.H. (Chairman) (1982) *Mathematics Counts* (Report of the Committee of Inquiry), HMSO, London.

DES (1979) *Mathematics 5-11: A Handbook of Suggestions*, HMSO, London.

DES (1987a) *Mathematics from 5 to 16: Curriculum Matters 3*, 2nd edition, HMSO, London.

DES (1987b) *The National Curriculum 5-16: A Consultation Document*, DES and Welsh Office, London.

DES (1988a) *National Curriculum: Task Group on Assessment and Testing: A Report*, DES and Welsh Office, London.

DES (1988b) *National Curriculum: Task Group on Assessment and Testing Report: A Digest for Schools*, DES and Welsh Office, London.

DES (1988c) *National Curriculum, Mathematics Working Group, Interim Report*, DES and Welsh Office, London.

DES (1988d) *National Curriculum, Mathematics for Ages 5 to 16*, DES and Welsh Office, London.

DES (1989) *Mathematics in the National Curriculum*, DES and Welsh Office, London.

HMI (1989) *Aspects of Primary Mathematics: The Teaching and Learning of Mathematics*, HMSO, London.

NCC (1988) *Mathematics: Consultation Report*, National Curriculum Council, London.

APPENDIX: CASE STUDIES

You may find it interesting to compare your work and your situation with that of others. We include three examples and the successes, problems and, as yet, unfulfilled aims may help you to see how others have attempted to develop this role. We are most grateful to the teachers who were willing to discuss their experiences as co-ordinators.

School A

In this junior and infant school the headteacher asked a member of staff from the infant department, whose role already included a responsibility for mathematics throughout the school, to undertake a one year part-time in-service course in mathematics education. The result was a change of role from head of the infants section to additional support teacher and mathematics consultant for the whole school.

This forward planning gave the teacher, the head and the school time to plan how the role could be successfully implemented. During the year the potential co-ordinator was able to develop the role, colleagues could observe and discuss the effects of the course and, importantly, the teacher was able to examine the changing relationship with her class that one day's absence a week caused. This helped with planning effective ways of preparing herself to work outside her own classroom.

After the course her timetable was arranged so that she could teach each class. This allowed non-contact time for the usual class teacher. The advantages of this arrangement were considerable but in practice it prevented the co-ordinator from working alongside the class teacher. The problem was partly because industrial action at the time made it very difficult to set up liaison between the staff. The co-ordinator organized a 'Mathematics Centre' which contained recent references and resources so that the staff had access to a much wider range of materials than had previously been the case. She made herself available to give support and advice to anybody who sought it. This developed, but a few members of staff still felt reluctant to discuss their mathematics curriculum with her.

Contact with the local education authority adviser was made at the beginning of the year and this proved to be very helpful and encouraging. He kept the co-ordinator in touch with developments. Regular meetings with co-ordinators from other schools have still to be established.

The response from the children has been very positive. Comments like 'maths can be fun' and 'maths does not have to be boring' bear witness to the impact the co-ordinator has made on the mathematics curriculum. One drawback this co-ordinator found was that being timetabled for one hour slots with each class tended to curtail many developments. Ideas being worked upon by her and the children had to wait a week. As she said, 'Children's minds do not work in one hour slots and neither does mine'. This reinforces the necessity for the co-ordinator to integrate closely with the class teacher.

As the year progressed the influence of the co-ordinator became more effective. Some problems were resolved during the year. Others will take longer to resolve but the influence that the co-ordinator is having will repay the effort involved.

School B

Here a class teacher was asked by the head to take responsibility for either mathematics or language. The teacher chose mathematics and has responsibility for the subject throughout the whole primary school. She asked to be allowed to attend a one year in-service course in mathematical education, the success of which she sees as having increased the strength of her role.

This co-ordinator is still a full-time class teacher of 39 first-year juniors. She does not get any time allowance to discuss mathematics with the staff or work alongside them.

Her immediate task as co-ordinator has been to prepare a mathematics curriculum which will broaden the approach to mathematics within the school from one closely adhering to their selected published scheme to one embracing more practical work, problem-solving etc. To achieve this she has prepared extra materials on investigations, problem-solving, logic and the calculator. These have been tried out with her own large class and a second-year class. They were then displayed in the resource area with an invitation to other teachers to use them freely.

Interest is growing, especially that of the headteacher, who has promised to take the co-ordinator's class and so give her time to work with other teachers. She has found the response of her colleagues most encouraging, although she has not been able so far to develop her ideas with the infant department.

The adviser has not yet met with her but she is keen to develop contact with him as she sees that his interest would increase the credibility of her role, keep her up to date with recent developments and help her to contact other co-ordinators.

The overall aim of this co-ordinator is to develop mathematics by her own example. She chose to use Dienes' apparatus with her class. Other teachers saw it on the children's desk, were impressed with the work the children were doing and consequently they decided to use it as well.

The initial organization in school B is quite different from school A but the enthusiasm and sound mathematical ideas developed are similar.

School C

The third teacher had responsibility for language throughout the school but her interests were in mathematics and science. When the mathematics co-ordinator left she was invited by the headteacher to take on this role. As with the other teachers in schools A and B she also attended an in-service course in mathematical education.

Again this teacher is a full time classroom teacher with no special time allowance. She finds it very difficult to implement her role. She has developed two main approaches. First, being available to offer advice, capitalizing on situations such as 'John has finished the maths scheme, what shall I do with him now?' which provide her with the opportunity to suggest ideas and new methods that might be tried. She also makes informal suggestions to colleagues 'have you tried this with your class?' Second, she organizes the school's mathematical resources, encouraging staff to share equipment and raising their awareness of what equipment is available within the school. This again leads to informal developments and it has been possible to hold workshop sessions in the school. She has also ensured that the staff were made aware of mathematics courses that were advertised in the area.

She has not made contact with the adviser yet but hopes to do so. He could be especially useful in assisting with the promotion of local and school-based in-service training.

Co-ordinators sometimes experience difficulty in encouraging the infant department to develop problem-solving investigations and calculator work. They frequently meet the response 'we cannot possibly do that with the infants'. This co-ordinator tackled the problem by spending some time in the infant department doing some investigational work. The results were that her colleagues saw how much the children gained from the approach, and she realized what their problems were and began to appreciate how different the approach was in the infant department. Again this emphasizes how important it is for the co-ordinator to be able to work alongside colleagues.

These three examples provide different approaches to implementing the role of the co-ordinator. They indicate both the support needed for the co-ordinator to function effectively and the major problems, especially the difficulties of finding adequate time to work alongside colleagues and to develop in-service work, and of motivating staff and pupils.

Organizing in-service activities is made much easier with the co-operation of the head. One school which wished to develop the use of the calculator managed it by the headteacher taking a whole school assembly so leaving the co-ordinator and the staff with time first to explore the calculator themselves and then to develop a whole school approach to using it. This required the headteacher to have confidence in the co-ordinator and to provide tangible support.

Sadly in some schools teachers have been nominated as mathematics co-ordinators but the only support they have is what they themselves have gained from attending in-service training (INSET) courses. While their enthusiasm for mathematics and the personal initiatives they have developed have a good effect in their schools they do need more support if they are to develop the quality of mathematics education in their schools.

2
MAKING A START

Introduction

Mathematics has been identified, along with English and Science, as forming the core of the National Curriculum and 'first priority will be given to these subjects' (DES, 1987b, paragraph 13). Why is mathematics considered to be such an important subject? What, indeed, is mathematics? Before devising detailed schemes of work you need to pay attention to these questions. As a starting point you might like to ask your colleagues for *their* definitions of mathematics and why *they* think it is an important subject. Alternatively you could collect a set of definitions of mathematics from encyclopaedias and mathematics books and use them as a way of starting discussion.

Why teach mathematics?

One thing is certain about mathematics teaching – there is a lot of it! The Cockcroft Report (1982) stated that junior classes devote about 5 hours a week to mathematics and that in most secondary schools all pupils up to the age of 16 take the equivalent of about five 35 minute periods per week. Thus mathematics can occupy as much as one-fifth of the teaching time in a junior school and between one-seventh and one-eighth of a teaching week in secondary school. Why so much time?

Mathematics 5-11: A Handbook of Suggestions (DES, 1979, p.3) when acknowledging that mathematics, at least in the form of arithmetic, has an important place in the education of young children says that 'the obvious reason for this is that numbers are part of everyday life and adults find it useful to calculate at work, while shopping and when engaged in sports and pastimes'. This basically utilitarian reason is frequently given as a justification for the place of mathematics in the school curriculum. However, as *Mathematics 5-11* points out, the skills necessary for these purposes can be acquired by most children by the time they leave primary school, so why not either treat mathematics as an optional subject in at least the upper forms of the secondary school or spread the mathematics curriculum more thinly over the primary and secondary stages? The first of these alternatives was seriously considered at one time but the advent of the National Curriculum has ruled out this possibility. However, there are reasons other than those of utility which can be put forward for the importance of teaching children mathematics.

The first chapter of the Cockcroft Report suggests some of these. They can be grouped under four main headings: utilitarian, cultural, educational, pleasurable.

Utilitarian	for everyday life; as already mentioned, the most often quoted reason for particular occupations – some pupils may require a thorough knowledge of maths for their eventual job
	for other subjects – some pupils may require a sound knowledge of maths to assist their study of other subjects, for instance science
Cultural	mathematics has played a major role both in the development of science and techology and of our, and other, civilizations
Educational	studying mathematics 'trains the mind' and assists the development of logical thought
	requires the development of a unique mode of thinking with its own cognitive structures
	assists in the development of spatial awareness
	provides the learner with 'a powerful means of communication – to represent, to explain and to predict'
	(Cockcroft, 1982, para. 8)
	fosters qualities of 'perseverance; imagination and flexibility; self-management and working skills; and, perhaps above all, a "can do" attitude to life's challenges'
	(DES, 1988, section 2.10)
Pleasurable	tackling mathematical puzzles may provide enjoyment and entertainment for some
	studying geometric patterns can stimulate aesthetic judgements
	solving mathematical problems can give 'the emotional satisfaction inherent in any creative exercise'
	(Gardner, Glenn and Renton, 1973, p.20)

It is difficult to justify the importance of mathematics on only one of these reasons. The reasons themselves are not independent, nor do they all solely apply to mathematics. Some other subjects can make the same claims. It is through a mixture of these reasons that the teaching of mathematics in schools, and its relative importance compared with some other subjects, can be justified.

It seems particularly unnecessary and ill-advised to justify the place of mathematics in the curriculum because of its uses in everyday life and in future employment. Many other subjects in the curriculum – English Literature, History and Geography, for instance – cannot be justified solely on utilitarian grounds and no-one tries to do so, so why should this be the sole justification for mathematics? The Mathematics Working Group emphasizes that mathematics is not only taught because it is useful: 'It should also be a source of delight and wonder, offering pupils intellectual excitement, for example, in the discovery of relationships, the pursuit of rigour and the achievement of elegant solutions' (DES, 1988, section 2.2).

You will form your own opinion as to the appropriateness and the relative importance of the various reasons listed above, but clearly some, for instance the contention that studying mathematics 'trains the mind', have to be treated with caution and do not easily lend themselves to empirical research methods as a means of support. Nevertheless, elements in the totality of reasons given would seem to justify the place of mathematics in the curriculum.

However, acceptance of anything more than purely utilitarian reasons presumes a definition of mathematics wider than a study of the techniques and skills necessary to deal with number, measurement and shape. For instance, mathematics as a way of communicating about the world can be considered to be of fundamental importance. This view was highlighted in the Cockcroft Report, which emphasized mathematics as a means of communication enabling one to represent, to explain and to predict. As the Mathematics Working Group says, 'in the broadest sense, mathematics provides a means for organizing, communicating and manipulating information' (DES, 1988, section 2.1).

What is mathematics?

How can one then define mathematics? How can a mathematical activity be distinguished from any other mental (or physical) activity? What does doing mathematics involve? These are very difficult questions to answer but before we can analyse critically the teaching of mathematics in primary schools or suggest a new curriculum or new teaching methods, it would seem necessary at least to consider these questions seriously and attempt to find partial answers.

Any attempt to define mathematics in a single, simple statement is bound to be inadequate, but analysing what one does when carrying out an activity generally recognized to be mathematical can help to provide some of the components of the mathematical process. Clearly these activities are generally carried out on mathematical 'objects'. At the primary level these 'objects' can generally be classified as numbers, measurements and shapes. The child must acquire some knowledge of these 'objects' (for example, begin to acquire the concept of number, identify symbols to represent numbers, establish the various relationships between numbers). Much of this knowledge is itself acquired through involvement in mathematical processes. What are these processes?

In order to begin to identify some of these processes, let us consider some elementary mathematical activities – all of which could be tackled by many junior school children.

1. Which of the following triangles are isosceles (Fig. 2.1)?

    Figure 2.1

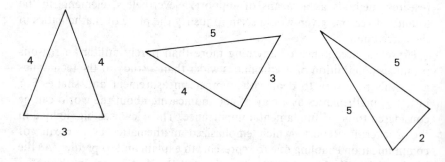

    Here the process is basically *classification*. Clearly the child must know something about the attributes of the objects under consideration. 'Sorting' is an accepted pre-number activity in infant schools.

2. Divide 136 by 8.

    Again some knowledge specifically about the 'objects' involved (for example, place value) is assumed. The actual process involved could be called *computation* and the result is obtained (probably) by the use of an *algorithm*. The result may be *checked* by, for instance, multiplication.

3. Can you find a way of working out how many cubes make up the box (Fig. 2.2)?

Figure 2.2

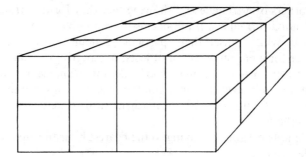

This may lead to the beginnings of a *generalized method* and hence to a *formula*.

4. What number is put into □ , if 2 × □ + 1 = 7?

Here we have the beginnings of algebraic representation, but *symbolization* of all sorts will have been met by primary children throughout their study of mathematics from their earliest infant days. To answer this question the child may initially begin with a *trial and error* method, but later a more systematic approach will be devised, based on the ideas of *logical deduction* (for example, 'whatever is deducted from one side must be deducted from the other').

5. Find the area of this shape (Fig. 2.3).

Figure 2.3

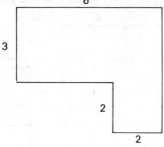

Clearly the use of a formula and computation will arise in this example, but to solve the problem the child (unless he draws it accurately and counts squares) will probably change the problem into a problem involving two areas (either added or subtracted). This is one example of *transformation* - changing a problem into an equivalent problem. Similarly to solve 3/4 + 1/6 he will transform the problem into 9/12 + 2/12.

6. Show that the angle sum of a triangle is two right angles.

At the primary level this will probably be demonstrated by tearing off corners of a triangle and showing that they form a straight angle. This is not a formal *proof* but begins to emphasize to the child the necessity to convince himself that a particular statement or relationship is *always* true for a particular set of objects, irrespective of which element of the set you consider. Formal proof is an important element of mathematics at a higher level. Primary children need to convince themselves of the general truth of certain mathematical statements by less formal methods.

7. Complete Table 2.1 giving to the nearest hour the amount of time each day you spend:

Table 2.1

	Hours
Sleeping	
Eating	
At school	
Watching TV	
Playing, etc.	

Illustrate your table.
Collection of data and *graphical representation* are important aspects of doing this.

8. The streets and avenues of Manhattan form a grid (Fig. 2.4).

Figure 2.4

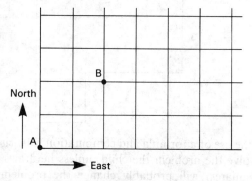

If you are at junction A, how many routes can you take to B (assuming that you do not turn back on yourself, so you are always heading east or north)? Find the number of routes to other junctions starting from A. Can you find a pattern for calculating the number of ways to a given junction from A?

This question incorporates an element of *modelling* (that is, simplifying the real-life situation to one which lends itself to a scientific or mathematical approach). Modelling is a very important aspect of 'real' mathematics. Understandably, because of the maturity and sophistication needed, it has not always been evident in mathematics taught to primary school children. However, with the development of new curricula initiatives in mathematics, modelling is now being explicitly experienced at an earlier age.

To solve the original problem requires devising a *procedure or algorithm* for generating the result for each junction.

9. On squared paper draw a rectangle five squares by six squares. Draw a diagonal of this rectangle. How many squares does the diagonal pass through?

Do this for other rectangles. Can you forecast the number of squares passed through if you know the length and width of the rectangle?

The solution to this problem will be a *generalization* expressed as a *formula*, enabling one to *predict* the answer for given data. To arrive at the generalization a good deal of data will be collected, probably initially in a haphazard way then, hopefully, more systematically by considering a *simplification* of the general problem (for example, you might start by looking at squares as a 'special' sort of rectangle). In a sense this simplification is a modelling procedure. All the time there is the search for *pattern* leading to a *relationship between variables*. 'Proof' is by *induction* (that is, the hypothesis is tested by checking with a number of miscellaneous examples).

Examples (1)–(7) involve taught techniques and procedures but (8) and (9) are more 'open-ended' problems. Traditionally, the emphasis in primary school mathematics has been on examples (1)–(7) – but more of this later.

Analysing the processes and techniques mentioned above, we can say:

1. Mathematics involves several general processes, including:
   (a) modelling
   (b) symbolization
   (c) classification
   (d) transformation
   (e) generalization

2. The strategy adopted to solve a mathematical problem may involve:
   (a) trial and error
   (b) using logical deduction
   (c) simplification of the problem
   (d) using induction
   (e) devising a hypothesis

3. Specific techniques used might include:
   (a) computation
   (b) simplification (algebraic or numerical)
   (c) measuring
   (d) using a known algorithm
   (e) using a known formula
   (f) collecting data
   (g) representing data graphically
   (h) looking for pattern
   (i) looking for relationship between variables

4. The solution to a mathematical problem may be expressed as either:
   (a) a specific result (number, measurement, etc.)
   (b) a generalization (formula, algorithm, or theorem)

5. Finally you have to convince yourself of the correctness of the solution, this may involve:
   (a) checking
   (b) proof: by informal methods; by formal mathematical methods

This list is not exhaustive, nor are the subsections independent of each other, but it does provide us with at least the beginnings of an answer to what is involved in doing mathematics.

Problem-solving

Clearly, what is written above suggests that much mathematical activity is to do with problem-solving.

Leone Burton (1984) labels the four stages of problem-solving as: entry, attack, review and extension. At the *entry* stage the problem-solver is explaining the problem and organizing and representing the information. Next the *attack* stage where strategies are adopted and various methods tried. These methods may involve certain mathematical skills and techniques. Then an acceptable resolution to the problem has to be formulated. It needs to be checked and possible extension or related problems examined. This is the *review/extension* stage.

All this may seem very remote from the diet of routine sums that used to make up the mathematics curriculum in a number of primary classrooms. However, tackling question (9) above for the first time most people will be involved in similar stages. (If you do not know the answer you may like to tackle the problem yourself before proceeding!)

There will be an initial stage of getting to grips with the problem, followed by an attempt to tackle the problem in a systematic fashion. Eventually you might formulate a hypothesis and this may come in a flash of inspiration or sudden insight. Your hypothesis will need to be checked and modified as necessary. Finally you may obtain a general result which you think fits and this you then check.

In terms of the processes and techniques mentioned earlier, solving question (9) could be analysed as follows:

Entry	*Modelling* the situation and representing the variables by *symbols*.
Attack	Initially *trial and error* but then a more systematic approach using, possibly, a *simplification* of the problem. The overall process will be an *inductive* one designed to derive a *hypothesis*.
	Collection of data, *calculation* and *looking for pattern* in order to find a *relationship* between variables.
Review/extension	A *generalization* expressed as a *formula*.
	Testing on miscellaneous examples – as already mentioned basically an *inductive* method.

So, although much of what has been said may seem too sophisticated for the primary classroom, many of the elements are present in situations accessible to children of primary school age.

Mathematics and the real world

If we accept this general view of what is involved in mathematical activity then we must also accept that mathematics is essentially a mental activity, and thus it is separate from the real world. Talk of 'mathematics in the environment' is nonsense. What does exist in the environment are certain phenomena and situations that lend themselves to mathematical analysis. Without the human mind mathematics would not exist.

How does mathematics relate to the real world? An Open University (1980) course *Mathematics Across the Curriculum* gives the following picture of this relationship (Fig. 2.5).

Figure 2.5

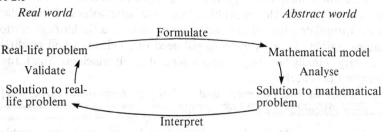

Thus the relationship is seen as a closed system but the school curriculum, in identifying separate disciplines, cuts through this diagram. If we consider that the right-hand side constitutes 'mathematics' then we see that the subject is concerned with formulating a mathematical representation (that is, model) of a real-world problem. This mathematical representation is then 'analysed' (that is, mathematical methods are applied to it) in order to provide a *mathematical* solution. This mathematical solution then has to be interpreted in terms of the original physical phenomena to provide a solution to the real-life problem. School mathematics, both at primary and secondary levels, has tended to ignore the formulation or modelling stage and the interpretation of the solution, and to emphasize the 'analysis' stage in isolation.

The result was that the vast majority of syllabuses considered only techniques applied to routine and stereotyped situations. Some of these techniques are specific (rules for computation, measurement, specific formulae and algorithms), others more general (sorting and classifying, searching for pattern, collecting data) but they are frequently dealt with separately, independent both of each other and of the general framework of the mathematical process. It is not surprising that a number of adults when looking back on school mathematics can find little in what they studied that appears relevant to either everyday life or to their work. Many also see mathematics as a collection of separate unrelated and incomprehensible 'tricks'. Indeed the Cockcroft Report (1982, paragraphs 20 and 22) besides noting that 'an apparently simple and straightforward piece of mathematics could induce feelings of anxiety, helplessness, fear and even guilt in some', also found that some 'felt a sense of inadequacy because they were aware that they did not use what they considered to be the "proper" method'. Laurie Buxton's book (1981) demonstrates only too clearly the 'panic' experienced by many adults when confronted with having to do some 'mathematics'.

The APU results (Assessment of Performance Unit, 1980) indicated that

11-year-old pupils have difficulty in applying mathematics to problems – they could cope with basic four-rule computation when presented as a 'sum' but not when it is to be used to solve a 'problem'. There are many reasons for this. The added difficulty of interpretation ('what does the question mean?') and the problems of reading obviously contribute, but another factor may be that for most children the primary mathematics curriculum was mainly about techniques and not about using mathematics to solve problems. Nor did children seem to recognize when they had a ridiculous answer: again partly because they never had to *use* the results of their calculation to solve a real-life problem. For some the impression gained is that mathematics is to do with sums but has little use in real life. The Mathematics Working Group (DES, 1988) has recognized this when it recommends as one of its attainment targets that

> Pupils should be able to select whatever mathematics is appropriate for the particular tasks, apply it sensibly and efficiently, try alternative strategies if needed, check on progress at appropriate stages, analyse the final results to ensure that initial requirements have been met, and complete the task.

Certainly computational skills and related number techniques *are* important. They do, after all, provide the basic tools by which many problems can be solved. However, competence in arithmetic is not sufficient in itself. There is certainly some evidence that rather too much time may have been spent in primary schools developing computational skills in isolation. The National Primary Survey entitled *Primary Education in England* (DES, 1978) said that 'in the classes inspected considerable attention was paid to computation, measurement and calculations involving sums of money' (paragraph 5.50) and that 'in about a third of the classes, at all ages, children were spending too much time undertaking somewhat repetitive practice of processes which they had mastered' (paragraph 5.55). The Scottish HMI's report (Scottish Education Department, 1980, p. 16):

> noted the fact that teachers continue to place a high value on the importance of arithmetic and an ability to handle the four processes accurately was evident in the survey: there was only one class where arithmetic was neglected. In 25 per cent, in the opinion of HM Inspectors, it was being over-emphasized.

As the Mathematics Working Group (DES, 1988, section 7.3) suggests,

> Real life problems, and the more demanding mathematical problems, of their nature do not come forward with a clear indication of the particular mathematics that they will require for their solution; nor will they necessarily draw on a narrow range of mathematics only.

Hence not only do pupils require knowledge of other areas of mathematics but also need to develop 'general strategies directed towards problem solving and investigations' (Cockcroft, 1982, paragraph 323). Even very young children can, and do, use some of these strategies. The Mathematics Working Group has identified some of the processes that one can expect pupils to begin to develop from a very early age. When referring to mathematics in the primary school, the Cockcroft Report (paragraph 321) suggests that

> All children need experience of applying the mathematics they are learning both to familiar everyday situations and also to the solution of problems which are not exact repetitions of exercises which have already been practised.

In recent years more textbooks and commercially produced mathematics schemes have included enrichment activities and investigations in their contents. Unfortunately the structure of some of the schemes means that these are seen by some teachers as 'extras' only to be tackled by the brighter children. As the National Curriculum documents make clear, tackling real-life problems and developing the necessary mathematical strategies should be seen as an integral part of the primary school mathematics curriculum.

Aims and objectives

What mathematics should be taught in primary schools? If one accepts that mathematics consists of more than just a set of specific skills and techniques, but that it involves the whole range of processes mentioned earlier, then two things follow. First, the amount of time devoted to mathematics in the primary school curriculum is justified; and second, the content of the mathematics curriculum must include this range of processes. One needs to have considered the nature of mathematical activity before it is possible either to criticize the content of existing curricula or to devise new ones. As Glenn and Sturgess (1977, p.11) say:

> For the majority of the children leaving the Primary School the most important asset they can have is experience of all kinds of mathematical activity and confidence in applying mathematical methods to the solution of problems.

These problems should not only be those imposed by the teacher but also the children's own problems.

What then are appropriate aims and objectives for mathematics teaching in the primary school? Hilary Shuard (1986) devised a four-dimensional model of the mathematics curriculum and this is discussed in detail in Chapter 6. However, when, as a co-ordinator, you are 'making a start' it will be worth your while looking at the aims set out in *Mathematics 5-11: A Handbook of Suggestions* (DES, 1979). Shuard gives the list of aims in the following shortened form:

1. a positive attitude to mathematics;
2. an appreciation of its creative aspects and an awareness of its aesthetic appeal;
3. ability to think clearly and logically in mathematics;
4. understanding through a process of enquiry and experiment;
5. appreciation of the nature of numbers and of space;
6. appreciation of mathematical pattern and relationships;
7. mathematical skills and knowledge;
8. awareness of the uses of mathematics beyond the classroom;
9. persistence through sustained work.

When considering objectives a useful source of ideas is *Mathematics from 5 to 16: Curriculum Matters 3* (DES, 1987a). In all, this lists 24 objectives for pupils in five categories. For your convenience these are given below.

Facts	remembering terms
	remembering notation
	remembering conventions
	remembering results
Skills	performing basic operations
	sensible use of calculator
	simple practical skills in mathematics
	ability to communicate mathematics
	the use of microcomputers in mathematical activities
Conceptual structures	understanding basic concepts
	the relationship between concepts
	selecting appropriate data
	using mathematics in context
	interpreting results
General strategies	ability to estimate
	ability to approximate
	trial and error methods
	simplifying difficult tasks
	looking for pattern
	reasoning
	making and testing hypotheses
	proving and disproving
Personal qualities	good work habits
	a positive attitude to mathematics

This list provides a valuable starting point. However, there needs to be a few words of caution. First, as you will have noticed, not all the items in the list are given explicitly in the form of objectives and need to be reworded appropriately (for example, 'pupils should realize when trial and error methods are appropriate and their limitations'). Second, the full meaning of the objectives can only be gleaned by reading the document itself. Third, the list provides an overall framework and it is for individual schools to put in the details which will depend on the children's ages, abilities and needs. It should be noted that the list is not just concerned with content but pays due attention to *processes* and to *attitudes*. These two aspects are fundamental to Shuard's model for the primary mathematics curriculum, which is considered in more detail in Chapter 6.

Summary

When making a start on looking at mathematics in your school, you need to consider several basic questions.

1. Why is mathematics thought to be such an important element in the school curriculum?
2. What is mathematics?
3. What are mathematical activities and processes?
4. How can problem-solving activities be introduced into the mathematics curriculum?
5. How does mathematics relate to the real world?
6. What are suitable aims and objectives for mathematics teaching?

You will need to discuss these questions with your colleagues and, as a group, you will naturally consider them in the context of your own situation. The next three chapters will help you to look at *your* school and *your* pupils.

References

Assessment of Performance Unit (1980) *Mathematical Development: Primary Survey Report*, no. 1, HMSO, London.

Burton, L. (1984) *Thinking Things Through*, Basil Blackwell, Oxford.

Buxton, L. (1981) *Do You Panic About Maths?* Heinemann, London.

Cockcroft, W.H. (Chairman) (1982) *Mathematics Counts* (Report of the Committee of Inquiry), HMSO, London.

DES (1978) *Primary Education in England* (A Survey of HM Inspectors of Schools), HMSO, London.

DES (1979) *Mathematics 5–11: A Handbook of Suggestions*, HMSO, London.

DES (1987a) *Mathematics from 5 to 16: Curriculum Matters 3* (2nd Edition), HMSO, London.

DES (1987b) *The National Curriculum: A Consultation Document*, DES and Welsh Office, London.

DES (1988) *National Curriculum, Mathematics for Ages 5 to 16*, DES and Welsh Office, London.

Gardner, K.L., Glenn, J.A. and Renton, A.I.G. (eds) (1973) *Children Using Mathematics*, Oxford University Press, London.

Glenn, J.A. and Sturgess, D.A. (1977) *Towards Mathematics*, Schofield and Sims, Huddersfield.

Open University (1980) *Mathematics Across the Curriculum*, Course PME 233, Open University Press, Milton Keynes.

Scottish Education Department (1980) *Learning and Teaching in Primary 4 and Primary 7* (A Report by HM Inspectors of Schools in Scotland), HMSO, Edinburgh.

Shuard, H. (1986) *Primary Mathematics Today and Tomorrow*, Longman for SCDC, York.

3
LOOKING AT YOUR SCHOOL

Introduction

Clearly, before you can take any initiatives in developing mathematics teaching, you must attempt to make some analysis of the current situation in your school.

You need to accept that all schools have strengths and weaknesses and these give the overall character of a particular school. Many different aspects combine to produce the school image. The staff and the parents are two important factors which affect the ethos of a school and you will need to consider their influences.

The staff (including yourself)

The interpersonal relationships of the staff are a vital part of the overall school ethos. We need to examine these relationships and recognize in a positive way how people interact, their strengths and weaknesses, their attitudes towards you and your attitude towards them. As mentioned in the Cockcroft Report, many teachers feel insecure about their own mathematics and are naturally reserved about discussing or undertaking curriculum developments suggested to them. Also many teachers are perceived by the head, parents and their pupils as highly successful mathematics teachers and these teachers may not feel the need to adopt changes and introduce the innovations you see as necessary.

We need to appreciate that because a colleague does not share our aspirations immediately this does not necessarily mean they are being difficult. Some colleagues will obviously be more responsive to suggestions and it is they who will be able to offer the immediate support needed when beginning the role of co-ordinator. Most staff can be encouraged to co-operate if we seek to approach them through their strengths. For instance, a teacher with a strength in art can use this as a way of developing their own mathematics. Likewise, they can help others to see the mathematics in art and this may enhance their own approach to teaching art.

Parents

Most parents show some interest in the school. Many teachers are parents and will understand and sympathize with the concerns parents express about the mathematics their children are learning. For many parents it was a subject of fear and one from which they gained little sense of achievement. Hence the sometimes emotive and irrational response that it arouses in them is quite understandable. As teachers we need to include parents in the development of the mathematics curriculum. We should try to answer their questions, be prepared to listen, discuss and help them.

Parents evenings, workshops and mathematics fairs enable parents to understand the learning experiences of their children. Parents can be invited into the classroom where they provide invaluable assistance in helping the teacher. This can help them to appreciate the mathematics that their children are doing.

While it is not unusual for parents to come into school to assist with art, craft, cooking and even reading it is still relatively rare for them to volunteer to help with mathematics and many would refuse outright if approached directly to do so. They can, however, often be more easily persuaded to assist in a games or investigational situation, and this can then be used as a basis to explain developments in the curriculum and to help them to understand the changing approaches to learning, recording and evaluating mathematics. Most parents can make a valuable contribution by relating mathematics to real-life situations and, in some instances, by providing specialist materials (see p. 129).

Finding out

If you are taking over the responsibility of mathematics co-ordinator in a school in which you have worked for some years, you may already have formed some ideas of how mathematics teaching is planned, resourced and taught. However, there are dangers in the situation. You may have picked up false impressions and you may have misinterpreted certain situations. You may be either too close to the situation or too concerned with day-to-day issues that the broader more fundamental issues are overlooked.

If you are appointed to another school then you must assess the situation as an outsider. There are advantages in this in that you approach the task with an open mind. However, you will have to work harder to obtain answers to your questions and you will have to assess the best way of acquiring these answers. The following sections suggest the questions you might ask and the means by which you might obtain answers. Some of the questions may require factual answers, while others are to do with attitudes, atmosphere and teachers' perspectives. The latter are more difficult to tie down and the answers you receive, from whatever source, will need to be interpreted by you, using your own judgement and in terms of the framework of the picture you are seeking to obtain.

What follows is a number of quesions that you might wish to address. They are not questions to which a definitive answer is easily found. Rather they are questions that may provoke and stimulate thoughts and actions and hence may provide a way into tackling the task of finding out more about mathematics teaching in your school.

Having identified situations or circumstances that you wish to change, or support or develop, you will need to plan and implement your strategies. You will need to evaluate the success or otherwise of your strategies as you progress and this ongoing, formative evaluation is considered in Chapter 11.

Aims and objectives

1.   Is there a mathematics scheme available?
2.   If so, are the aims of the scheme clearly defined?
3.   Are the aims sufficiently comprehensive (see Chapter 2, page 29)?
4.   Is a published textbook scheme is use?
5.   If so, is there a commentary on the scheme which explains its aims and rationale?
6.   Are the objectives for each topic clearly defined?
7.   Are the objectives expressed in terms of the pupils' learning?
8.   Do the objectives cover processes and attitudes as well as content?
9.   Do the objectives provide the teacher with a better understanding of what content and approach is appropriate?
10.   How do individual teachers interpret, and use, the aims and objectives?

Most of these questions can be answered by looking at the available documentation but you will need to talk to your colleagues about how they interpret the aims and objectives and whether they think they are appropriate.

Children's needs

1. Are the children's needs in mathematics being identified?
2. Are these needs documented?
3. Do the aims of the mathematics curriculum fulfil the children's needs?
4. Is the curriculum relevant to the children's needs?
5. Are there specific difficulties that some of your children might encounter?
6. Is the language used in the scheme appropriate to the children?
7. Is the material sufficiently motivational?
8. Does the content and organization of the scheme cope with the extremes of ability?

Finding answers to these questions is a daunting task and you must not expect to reach precise answers. However, the very act of striving to obtain answers should help you to clarify your own opinions on how best to satisfy the needs of the pupils. You must bear in mind not only the views of your colleagues but also be prepared to consider the opinions of parents.

Most importantly, you obtain feedback from the pupils: try to ascertain what they perceive as being important, relevant and enjoyable.

Curriculum content

1. Is there a comprehensive coverage of topics?
2. Is the content in line with the National Curriculum Programmes of Study?
3. Is there sufficient material at each of the levels of attainment?
4. Does the scheme enable the more gifted children to develop mathematically?
5. Is there sufficient varied content to interest and motivate the less able children?
6. Is there opportunity for pupils to develop their own problem-solving strategies?
7. Does the scheme provide a sensible balance between processes, facts and skills?
8. Is investigational work an integrated part of the scheme?
9. Is sufficient attention being placed on the use of calculators and computers?

There is a considerable amount of material written about the content of the primary mathematics curriculum and the essential items, in broad terms, have been set out in the National Curriculum. Some of the issues are discussed in Chapter 6, and the task of choosing a published mathematics scheme or of devising your own scheme is considered in Chapter 8. The references and bibliography suggests further reading in this area which you might wish to undertake.

To help you answer some of the above questions, it is often useful to compare the content of your scheme with that of other schools. Try to obtain information from other schools (and visit them if possible), seek the advice of your mathematics adviser and see if there are any suitable courses available.

Teaching styles and organization

1. What forms of classroom organization are being used?
2. Are the teachers using a variety of teaching styles (for example, group work, discussion, investigational and project work)?
3. Are teachers aware of the aims and objectives of the scheme?
4. Do they *support* the aims and rationale of the scheme?
5. Do they know where to seek advice and find additional resources?
6. Have individual teachers particular strengths or weaknesses in mathematics teaching?
7. Is mathematics seen as an important component in cross-curricular projects?
8. Are your colleagues able to come into your classroom to observe you teaching mathematics?

To answer these questions you will need to talk to your colleagues and your headteacher. You will need to observe the teachers in their classrooms. This requires tact and sensitivity on your part. It is very important that your colleagues should realize that, as professionals, they have much expertise and experience that, if shared, can help in the overall aim of improving mathematics teaching in their school.

Resources

1. What resources has your school for mathematics teaching?
2. Are these resources readily available to all members of staff who will require them?
3. Are the resources stored in a way that they can be used efficiently?
4. Which resources are in high demand but short supply?
5. What resources are needed but not available?

Some of these questions can be answered by making an inventory and by analysing the use of resources as demanded by the scheme. You will also need to observe how the resources are being used – and, as always, you will need to consult with your headteacher and with colleagues.

Physical environment

1. How is each classroom and its resources organized?
2. Are there suitable areas for practical mathematics in individual classrooms or is there a suitable area elsewhere?
3. Is there an obvious place that could be used for a whole school display or workshop area?
4. How is the environment in and around the school being used mathematically?

The ultimate aim is to assess the environment so that we can utilize it to promote the mathematics curriculum. Every school is different and if you are coming into a new situation you may see, through fresh eyes, how the physical environment may be hindering the teaching of mathematics or how it could be utilized more profitably. If you have been in the same school for some years then familiarity may make it more difficult to see the potential of the environment. In this case visiting other schools may alert you to new possibilities.

Record-keeping

1. Is there an adequate record-keeping system available?
2. What is the purpose of this system?
3. Does the system satisfy the national assessment procedures?
4. Are the records being used sensibly?
5. Do all members of staff use the system in the same way?
6. Is the system comprehensive, but not too time-consuming?
7. Are profile reports for each pupil compiled each term?
8. Does it provide the opportunity quickly to identify pupils' difficulties?
9. Is it based on recording children's understanding or merely topics experienced?
10. How are the results relating to pupils' personal qualities being recorded and incorporated into profile components?

Any record-keeping system needs to be a help rather than a burden to teachers. It must be informative but concise and easily understood by all members of staff and, of course, should meet the requirements of reporting for national assessment. We discuss this further in Chapter 10.

Evaluation and assessment

1. How do teachers evaluate their own mathematics teaching?
2. How is the effectiveness of the mathematics curriculum evaluated?
3. How is pupils' performance assessed?
4. Have agreed forms of assessment by teachers (TA) been established?
5. Do assessment arrangements encourage teachers to implement the national mathematics curriculum?
6. Are assessments being made against each of the appriopriate national attainment targets?
7. How does this assessment relate to any locally agreed testing procedures?
8. Do the assessment methods reflect the teaching approach?
9. Can the pupils' assessments be used diagnostically?
10. Does the assessment cover processes and concepts as well as facts and techniques?
11. What consideration is given to assessing pupils' attitudes and perseverance?
12. How is a pupil's ability in problem-solving and investigational work assessed?

Answering these questions will give you some idea of the effectiveness of your school's evaluation and assessment procedures. The introduction of national assessment arrangements and, in particular, the place of teacher assessment (see Chapter 1) within these arrangements has further increased the importance of this area. Indeed, evaluation and assessment, both of a school's teaching and of pupil performance, is central to the co-ordinator's job, so a detailed consideration of these aspects is given in Chapters 10 and 11.

Change

In answering all of the questions above you must be realistic. Equally you must be realistic if you wish to bring about change. There is the danger of expecting to change too much too quickly. Many people in many fields of education can testify that changes in the curriculum and in teaching methods take many years to implement. Once you have identified a problem or task to tackle then you must be prepared to break it down into manageable component items, if you are to attain your goal.

Patrick Easen (1985) gives a number of hints and strategies that may help you if, as a result of looking at your school, you wish to bring about change. He stresses the need to:

1. Consider constraints – because your problem does not exist in a vacuum.
2. Formulate the problem appropriately – so that it is at a level in which action can be taken.
3. Generate a wide range of ideas for tackling the problem – to avoid 'tunnel vision'.
4. Break the problem down into manageable parts – so that you can see a way forward for tackling it.

Looking at your school, if done sensitively and with a genuine desire to identify the strengths as well as the weaknesses of the situation, can have many long-term benefits. The aim should always be to use the information gleaned to help you to improve the mathematics teaching in your school. Looking at your school in this way will raise many issues and the following chapters look at some of these in more detail.

Summary

When looking at your school you must not overlook the importance and influence of staff and parents.
Look at:

1. Aims and objectives
2. Children's needs
3. Curriculum content
4. Teaching styles and organization
5. Resources
6. Physical environment
7. Record-keeping
8. Evaluation and assessment

Whatever changes such an analysis suggests, you must be realistic when tackling the problems.

Reference

Easen, P. (1985) *Making School-Centred INSET Work*, Open University/Croom Helm, Milton Keynes/London.

4
CHILDREN'S NEEDS: GENERAL ISSUES

Introduction

Unlike the teachers in many countries where quite a detailed outline is laid down centrally for all children and the teachers must just implement the plans, even when working within the guidance of a National Curriculum we face daily the task of assessing our children's needs. One of our greatest assets as British educators is this freedom we have as class teachers to decide – within broad frameworks – on the content of our lessons, even though it puts on us the enormous responsibility of deciding what this content should be. No two children are quite alike, and the range of variation we find in almost every class is enormous.

As primary teachers we have the responsibility of providing learning situations and experiences for individual pupils, albeit within the context of class projects, topics or themes. The National Curriculum provides only a framework which 'leaves ample scope for teachers to use professional expertise to adjust teaching approaches and the selection of examples and materials to the needs and circumstances of individual pupils' (DES, 1988, section 10.12). So how can we tell just what to provide for each child's needs? What are the questions we must ask ourselves?

In this chapter we look at some of the general issues that need to be considered when deciding on a child's educational needs. In the next chapter we look in more detail at special groups of children.

Relevance and home background

First, how does this class compare with those we have recently been teaching? Is what we have generally in mind relevant to Carol and Ahmed and Sean and Surinder? How much meaningful experience have they already had with language, activities, relationships, notation and symbolism, numbers and shapes? Are there sufficient common factors to form small working groups, and to formulate general provision? What variations must we make, and for which individuals within this group? Our answers will depend importantly on the home backgrounds, attitudes and standards. Do we know as much as we might about what 'our' parents are thinking? Would they agree with us? Are their feelings for mathematics those of deeply ingrained fear with very negative memories? Is the child struggling against this attitude, or, perhaps, achieving reasonable results in his work at school but not really able to share his experiences at home? Or is the child perhaps showing abilities far in excess of what the background would suggest, with consequently little understanding of his parents' reactions to his work? What implications are there here for our planning? We have discussed in Chapter 3 some aspects of parent–teacher relationships as seen in various types of meetings.

Alternatively it may be that the parents of some of our children are at the other extreme – very able mathematicians working in some academic field or with considerable industrial or educational experience. Sometimes in this situation we may find their children's mathematical development well appreciated and understod at home and steadily encouraged; but on the other hand, we may find the child put under the pressure of most inappropriate expectations. If so, it may be particularly hard to fend off this excessive pressure, especially if we are feeling the limitations of our own abilities! This is when we must remember that we are the professionals whose expertise lies in helping our pupils to develop their own potentialities. In these circumstances it is particularly important to be on genuine discussion terms with the parents, perhaps to show them how and why aproaches have changed over the years or that we are striving for the same ends.

We may find that a number of parents still have surprisingly little knowledge of what to expect in school and lack an understanding of the methods used and of the route we choose to follow to help the children attain understanding. We may need to do more 'explaining' to the parents than to our pupils! The latter will follow our lead, and hopefully will sometimes jump ahead of us, providing we are leading through real experiences, dealing with meaningful situations, and using well-understood language while extending it steadily as becomes appropriate.

Besides these home-environmental factors, the relevance of mathematical notions clearly varies according to age and general intellectual maturity. Here we have to remember that having a 'norm' implies that it is absolutely normal for many children to have advanced further and for many to have progressed less far along any particular path. By definition, half the group is below average for that group, and only half above. Besides this we know that few children develop steadily in any direction: most will progress at quite different rates now and again, sometimes taking an astonishingly long time to consolidate certain notions which others take in their stride, and at other times seeming to sweep aside what others find difficult, and to leap ahead, perhaps even with several ideas at once. Frequently children who have grasped more advanced notions need to return to consolidate apparently simpler ones which have been bypassed or skipped over.

How often we meet those pupils who seem to flit from idea to idea, and how pleased we are to find those whom we describe as having 'stickability', who persist and struggle on until they have truly mastered their task! But are we sometimes letting them struggle with something for too long at a time? When should we call it off for a bit? It may well be a tone of voice which becomes dulled, or a greater interest in a neighbour's work that tells us to suggest a change even before completion of a particular section. How soon then should we return to the previous task? Quite soon, perhaps, or next day, or even later than that. How boring our job would be if the answer to this question were always the same! On the other hand how can we get the 'flitters', the butterflies, to settle long enough to reach the nectar, and what is the equivalent for Laura, say, of the attractively bright petals that will stimulate her appetite for that particular sip of learning? With what other apparatus and in what fresh situation can we re-present the same or a similar notion to the one over which the struggle is taking place or the enthusiasm being turned off?

Some aspects of motivation

Practical work and co-operative approaches

This is our next important question: how can we motivate our pupils? Mathematics, perhaps above all subjects, must involve the whole person of the child – body, mind, emotions and aesthetic sensibilities. Physical experiences of handling apparatus in a great variety of shapes, sizes, forms, colours, textures are as important as work with patterns of shapes, of numbers and of movements. All these are very conducive to enjoyment.

These are closely allied to the satisfying emotion of 'It's mine', 'I did it', 'I thought it', or as one child put it, 'It was my own think'. This need for stimulus to think provided by concrete objects persists well beyond the infant and lower junior school stages where it is often more readily accepted. If we wean our children too completely from using physical models and apparatus we deprive them not only of a fundamental need to share a discovery but also of an important means of communicating ideas for which they have not yet acquired a verbal language. Also a genuine source of imaginative stimulation to generate new ideas is lost. For many children nowadays this may well also come from activities with calculators and/or computers, or from some investigative puzzle or problem-solving situation: these also lend themselves well to developing mathematical language.

One danger in working abstractly is that it is only too easy to assume something 'works' or 'fits' or has a certain size or value, whereas testing it out with real objects or the apparatus will at once display that this is wrong and may well simultaneously suggest an alternative approach. Even more importantly, it contributes to the sound thinking arising from knowing positively 'I am right' and enables the child to say without loss of self-esteem 'I thought so and so but I was wrong: I should have done this instead'. How much better this is than any 'outsider' saying 'No, that's wrong' and damaging, if not quite destroying, self-respect and confidence in thinking.

Perhaps it is as thought-provokers or motivators that we see the greatest value of calculators and computers for young children. They may use them as sources of exploration, discover their own logic and match what happens there with other aspects of their real life. Further advantages of the use of apparatus, models, calculators and so on show in the extent to which they encourage co-operation. Some children do indeed find competition a stimulus, but these may well not be those who need it most! Perhaps also it need not, even for them, be as all-pervading as is sometimes the case. Surely co-operativeness is increasingly more important in the world today, as shown in the increased development of institutionalized research.

On the personal level, too, co-operative working not only promotes greater enjoyment but also leads more often to higher achievement by all the children than any of them as individuals would otherwise experience. Through the need to explain to partners what you are thinking and trying to do, a deeper understanding of the situation under consideration develops and a clearer, more precise 'picture' is often achieved. We can also encourage co-operation through working on a 'topic', assuming this means more than individuals working alone on separate aspects of the chosen theme. A small group can, through discussion, extend each other's appreciation of a problem and understanding of the inherent mathematics, as well as seeing the mathematical notions in relation to real-life situations and other aspects of the curriculum.

We know well that some of the most exciting moments in teaching come with the original suggestions children make that we had never envisaged and with the new ways they can look at some of our old ideas. Often we need to hold ourselves back from suggesting too much initially as this can close off unexpected avenues in their embryo stages. Where our suggestions seem essential, perhaps at a frustrating impasse, it is preferable to give alternative possibilities for the children to choose and pursue, rather than to 'tell' them what to do.

Workcards

Not only do our children grow from hour to hour, absorbing unknown influences in the playground or dining-room as well as at home, but also we are changing daily in what we can appreciate of their mental growth. We must not risk nullifying this growth, so a useful structure is to introduce the basic notion being tackled through a simple activity that any child in the group can do without having to clamour for help or sink into frustrated despair. Then extend this with some more demanding idea/activity and end with an open situation to be tackled at very different levels and in varying depth according to each child's ability. In order to cope with these different levels you may feel that it is appropriate to use workcards or assignment sheets.

There are several important points to bear in mind when using workcards. Have we checked lately that our workcards can all be understood by those children who are to use them? Have we looked at the size, spacing and type of lettering used as well as the choice of vocabulary, the complexity of language and the extent of the content? It may be a false economy to be overthrifty with the margins at the sides, and the spaces at the top and bottom, as they allow the card to be held in whatever way the child finds comfortable without obscuring information or instructions. Do the illustrations help the reading, provide structure for the work, clarify the activities to be carried out and improve the presentation – or are they just a gimmick? We should also avoid crude illustrations. Those of us who are not natural artists may find the use of pin-people effective in stating a procedure. The standard of presentation of the card sets the tone for how the child approaches the work and how he/she presents his/her own work. Workcards should involve activities, not merely 'sums' for practice! They may indicate a source of examples or practice exercises but these should be a vital part of, or outcome from, the activity, and not added for their own sake.

We may design workcards in order to consolidate new vocabulary recently introduced in discussion, with an exploration or activity to reinforce the meanings. It may sometimes be advisable to list the equipment needed, so that it may be collected first to avoid breaking the continuity of the thinking in progress, but sometimes deciding what to use may be part of the fun and the challenge. Although we may often deem it wise to state that the results obtained are to be recorded, it is not usually profitable to impose rigid formats. It is a more profitable exercise to allow pupils to develop their own ways of recording and then to discuss the relative merits of the various systems of notation, rather than impose on them a standard symbolism which they may not fully comprehend.

Some cards will, of necessity, be of transient value, so we do not want to make it too hard for ourselves to scrap these! Those of a permanent nature need to be covered or varnished once they have proved their worth, for there are enough hindrances to learning without being put off by tatty and grubby cards. Avoid making two cards exactly alike, for if there is some slight variation between two it may promote individual effort and provide further practice at the same level. Similar, but different cards can be used for comparison by asking 'does your way work for this one too?' Or they can provide profitable occupation for a few moments while waiting to see you.

Finally it is useful to keep handy some blank cards ready cut, and the necessary pens, so that revision or extension cards, or a pilot card for a sudden idea, can be made quickly. You may not be able to devise enough cards from your own ideas and those of your friends and colleagues; then you will need to look at the possibility of cannibalizing a single copy (or perhaps two if you want both sides of the page) of a book you no longer need. Pages cut out may enable you to have more in use at any one time, enable you to discard unwanted bits, bring parts up to date, or adapt parts as children develop their own ideas. The intention is to be thoughtful and flexible, and to avoid prolonged isolation for any child.

Enjoyment

We have mentioned earlier in this chapter the importance of the joy of achieving personal success in thinking and of a child having his/her own ideas – ideas new to that child. For enjoyment in learning is a vital element of education, without which we do not engage the whole personality in the learning process. It is intrinsically linked to success, since zeal will carry a learner over an awkward stumbling block or difficulty, while continuing failure is a sure killjoy and often a complete road-block to progress. So we see how important it is for each one to build up steadily increasing confidence in his own working and thinking. Enjoyment also comes from experiencing fundamentally attractive visual, textural and kinaesthetic materials and apparatus. Such experience may be provided, for example, by encouraging young children to sort materials – simple things like feathers, rings of varying materials, small smooth and brightly coloured plastic toys of many types, beautiful dolls dressed in varying colours and textures.

We need to use an enormous variety of stimulants to engage the perceptions of children so that they acquire the foundations of set concepts and language, and are led into the basic relationships of weighing and measuring. At the same time they need to develop the language and writing skills needed to move from simple picture recording and words to their own symbolic notation. Eventually will come an appreciation of and then facility in standard symbols and notational forms. All the time we should be establishing sound attitudes towards mathematical learning as a whole. Language representation and use of symbols are discussed in more detail later.

Another source of enjoyment is the fun of real surprise. Perhaps after several things have fitted straightforwardly into a pattern of experience and recording we meet one that 'doesn't quite work', which makes us think again and extends our ideas. How important it is not to throw out the example that does not quite fit! Not only are we introducing thereby a false simplicity but we take away the option of deciding what to do about it, and how to reformulate the rules, which is an essential part of true mathematics.

It may sometimes be very trying to us as teachers seeing clearly a defined goal ahead to meet the child who wants to do 'his own thing'! This is when we call on our professionalism which demands that we detect the possibilities in the children's own ploys and lead these to the fullest possible development. We may have to leave aside for a while an important mathematical notion but, if it really is important there will be ample opportunities of meeting the essential fundamental notions in another guise later. With the assimilation of new ideas into a previously established schema of knowledge comes new enjoyment and more sophisticated understanding.

These approaches do, of course, demand time which is a vital factor for enjoyment. It takes time to make an experience or some knowledge one's own, time to understand and to put into words or pictures, and then, perhaps, to symbolize these for future use. This implies plenty of time for familiarization, absorption, accommodation (by use) and 'digestion' before automatic use can be expected. It is when these early and, what to the teacher may seem easy, stages of any notion are rushed that later confusions are spawned. Then all enjoyment of aspects connected with this experience is stifled, and once 'turned off' the rekindling of enjoyment and consequently the remotivation is far more difficult. Further, time spent in becoming completely at home with any new notion is amply repaid by the greater speed at which later steps in the more advanced processes are absorbed, and we avoid time-wasting on back-tracking. A common reply among those of us following syllabuses to those wanting to innovate is 'Yes, but we haven't time', so it is reassuring to find that this extra time given to beginnings and the introduction of new notions is not wasted but invested to be repaid with interest.

Encouraging children's abstraction

Most classrooms have sets of apparatus like Colour Factors, or Logibloks but are they lying unused in the cupboard for all or most of the time? If so, were they just considered a 'bandwagon' that has rolled by or have we been too busy with the next items to make use of those we already have? Perhaps we have tried these materials and found success needed more understanding of their possibilities than either we or the children have had time to attain. We surely need to make the best of all opportunities for letting our groups explore the concepts of number, shape and relations. Maybe having grown past the commercial pressures of these materials we may use them all to apply the essence of Dienes' 'variability principles', and to realize how important it is to explore each notion with variations of shape, size, position, deformability, colour and texture. We may need also to pursue a particular notion in relation to other numbers, or other closed polygons, or in three as well as two dimensions, and to see what happens if they are cut or put together, if they form tessellations, and how they relate to numbers and number patterns. Depth of understanding may often be obtained by 'repeating' a pattern or process in or with two or three different types of materials and apparatus.

You may have met adults who can only think of numbers as domino patterns or in some other set form which was the sole visual representation from which they learned their early number work. We must beware that we are offering too few forms of representation, with the danger that true generalization and abstraction are made far more difficult than need be. During all this activity how can we tell what is going on in a child's mind? We have already suggested that one of the important aspects of manipulating small apparatus is that it enables the child to express his thoughts in a real and precise way. This allows both other children and the teacher to see what he is 'saying', and so helps to develop language by moving from representational drawings to some form of symbols. Following experiences leading to the recognition, without counting, of the cardinality of a small number of objects we can then lead the child to form small sets which requires 1–1 matching of number names and objects and hence the skill of counting.

Language

Mathematical language grows, like everyday language, through continual nourishment in situations where the child is interested, and sometimes excited by what is going on around him/her and what he/she is doing. So it will develop through stages of naming and doing to classifying. Hearing language leads to copy-use and then to attempts to use the terms themselves. They become both increasingly more widely employed and more precisely chosen with increasing experience. There is an analogy with gardening here as the use of language is encouraged by preparing the ground, 'sowing seeds' of names or 'planting' terms. Development is fed and nourished by presenting situations that extend the use of language and introduce new words and constructions.

Children clearly show a need to understand an activity or notion and to fix it with names. An infant in the hall of a school seeing a visitor as he passed through called out 'what's your name?' Without stopping he turned his head to receive the reply, said 'Oh' as he accepted this 'label' and passed on, satisfied. With names fixed, a child will go on to express what he has observed in his own words, drawings or actions to relate them to each other and to his already familiar world, and then to communicate these to others – sometimes to anyone handy who will look and/or listen. It is often astonishing how much is then remembered, sometimes very much later. The very act of formulating ideas for communication can promote a clarification of details.

Involvement in discussion leads to a need to learn and then to use a neighbour's mode of communication, and ultimately to progress to appreciating standard expressions. Indeed, young children love real names and, if they are long, 'play' with the sound of the word. Try ignition, carburettor, parallelogram, hexagonal prism, and even parallelepiped! We detect a similar line of development towards the use of symbols through pictures, 'nicknames' and then a shorthand for words at first, but later embodying their own notions and eventually becoming entities in their own right. So manipulation of familiar everyday objects, with later manipulation of pictures and more abstract or representative apparatus, leads on to the children's use of words and then of symbols – initially particular ones but advancing to more generalized symbols and, in time, to an abstraction of the composite notion that the symbol represents.

The number symbols we write are just squiggles to infant children until they have acquired the concepts of one-ness, two-ness, three-ness. Counting is merely a jingle until the child can match number sounds with objects and can realize the significance of what he is doing. A child playing at spaceship launching may chant 'Ten, nine, eight, seven, six, five, four, three, two, one, zero, blastoff' before he is able to count. He has a clear sense of the order of the sounds, but this is just one of the elements involved in understanding numbers.

Besides the ordering of the sounds, ordering is such an important concept in mathematics that it, too, needs to be experienced in a great variety of contexts. Some situations involve cycles, like days of the week, and months of the year, with dates/numbers now overlapping, now coinciding, and so on – all part of the bigger game of looking for patterns and series. These more advanced notions come more readily to children who have ordered fir cones by eye and by measurement with calipers; strings and ribbons according to length, thickness/breadth and colour; buttons by diameter and number of holes; themselves by ages, heights and weights. Many of these activities need not initially use numbers. When 'measuring children' we need to take care, however, that no child loses esteem by being considered extreme in any way. Is the smallest best for a character in a play, can the tallest reach a high shelf best, will the heaviest be best for flattening a pile of papers? Does ordering according to different criteria given the same results? As well as clarifying aspects of 'bigness' according to varying forms and qualities, we can ask, for example, 'Has the largest ball the longest "roll"?' or 'Is it the same for the largest wheel?', so preparing the way for more advanced notions such as appreciating π as a ratio factor or multiple. If so, is this mere coincidence or is there a reason for the similarity? How can we express this reason? Considerations of order also lead naturally to discussions of 'more' and 'less' and involve notions of addition and subtraction. Children need to experience the operations of addition and subtraction in a variety of contexts and they need to hear the many linguistic structures we use in everyday speech for each operation. Only then can the general terms of 'addition' and 'subtraction' be introduced.

Subtraction may be introduced parallel with addition but it will probably be the first inverse mathematical process met explicitly. It is much more abstract than the operation of addition which can easily be seen physically as putting together either discrete objects, lengths, or weights on a scalepan and so on. Discrete objects can indeed be 'taken away'. We can cut off a piece of string or ribbon, and lift (or pour) something out of a scalepan, but it is another process to measure what we have taken away and what we have left. Furthermore, it is often a 'find the difference' situation that calls for subtraction. 'How much heavier am I than you?' demands that I 'take' one weight from the other, but, alas, that does not help me to lose any weight . . . . It is not taken away. We are dealing here with higher orders of abstraction. Again, 'How much more flour do I need?' and other similar questions are usually answered by adding on. This is a matter of the child's experience as we are dealing with several different processes. These will be seen eventually to come together as different facets of a process called 'subtraction'. It seems, however, dangerous and most unwise to use this term before the recognition of the overall process has taken place. The danger lies in the likelihood of the term being firmly linked to just *one* aspect. It may be better to use the words that truly describe the process until the inverse relationship with addition is realized in each case, and the sameness of all is perceived.

What does this imply for our language as a teacher? Apart from encouraging both wide use of language and discussion between children and between teacher and child, we must watch our own use of words. We must avoid limiting our language to stereotypes, but use correct mathematical terms as soon as this reduces ambiguities and contributes to clear thinking and expression.

How do we correct a child in the classroom? What effect might we have if we tell a child he is 'wrong'? The child loses his teacher's approbation, goes down in his peers' esteem and even more in his/her own. Worse still he may assume he was totally wrong when in fact he was almost right. Even more devastatingly he may be giving a perfectly correct answer to a question either heard as totally different from that which the teacher thought she had asked or, perhaps, genuinely misinterpreted. Now the child is told that 'right' answer is wrong – very confusing, this business of learning! If on the other hand we say 'Can you explain why?' or 'Show me why you think that', or even 'Do the rest of you agree with this?', the ensuing discussion will show the argument, and explain the thinking to, and of, other children. This surely deepens the understanding of all, and builds up confidence generally.

Often we use language in a misleading or ambiguous way, for example 'What can you say about the size?' Pictures of objects can be misleading. An object may look big against an undefined background, whereas in reality it may be tiny.

What non-standard language is used by children, and what does it reveal of their thinking? 'A second half' is not uncommon for a quarter and we must surely all have our own favourite examples. On the other hand, how do children see our standard language? When we take for granted words unfamiliar to our listeners, they probably do one of two things: they either ignore the word and hence do not listen to that phrase, or they substitute a similar sounding well-known word and try to make sense of that.

Are there also questions that are better, or worse, than others? Are some more useful, more motivating? Are any hiding dangerous pitfalls? Try jotting down some of the questions you find yourself asking, or record yourself chatting with a group, and them chatting together subsequently. On listening to it afterwards you may be surprised!

Do some very particular questions seem essential in very particular situations? Are there any that are applicable in many diverse situations? Useful questions in the latter category are 'Does that always work?', 'What happens if . .?' and 'Can you still do that if . .?' These turn attention to the boundaries of a situation, and by exploring extremes we can often establish the definition of the concept in question.

Again there are *demotivating* statements and question, such as 'Yesterday you knew . . .', or 'Last week you could do that' which can destroy confidence if the point of view has changed now or if other topics are now uppermost in the child's mind! An alternative approach is 'Try to remember what you did with these pieces yesterday' or 'Where have you seen something like this before?' or 'Try and look at this again in another way. What else can you do?' A child may need to do again several times exactly what he did 'yesterday' before he realizes its import, even though this is 'obvious' to others. Another child may need variations to perceive what is really lying behind his actions and their results.

We really must not be in too much of a hurry for a solution to be spotted! When puzzling how to solve a particular problem you may need to come back to it again and again on different days before suddenly 'seeing' the solution! What triggers the ultimate solution may be difficult to tie down, but you will probably want to reach this solution yourself without outside help. We need to keep reminding ourselves how important such personal success is for young learners, and how much they then need to tell someone else all about it.

Symbolism

We have referred above to the necessity of taking plenty of time, even if the available time seems short, over the early stages of any new concept or process. This is important for all learning and all pupils. Ideas may seem so simple to us as teachers that, after going over the ground with class after class for several years, each time improving our technique and so cutting down on the 'practice' required, we tend to forget how new the concept may be for the child and how necessary is time for him to 'digest' the notion. This is no less true when children are developing new notation or symbolism.

Place value is a much higher-order concept than those likely to have been encountered in arithmetic up to that time. The use made of notation is very central to the concept. Children will quite happily use words like 'eleven', 'twelve', and so on in the sequence of counting numbers without necessarily relating them in any way to ten, or appreciating how our method of notation enables us to build up such a powerful means of recording numbers and operating with them.

Various stages need to be passed through if the concept of place value and the resulting system of symbolization is to be understood:

1. an understanding of cardinality, as the common element of equivalent sets, irrespective of the type, size and colour of objects in the sets – thus the commonality of *three* toys and *three* pencils is their 'three-ness';
2. an awareness that a set can be split, or partitioned, into subsets (important also to the concept of addition);
3. the knowledge that a standard way of partitioning a set is to collect subsets of ten;
4. the use of the number names to describe such sets in terms of the subsets (for example, two subsets of ten and a subset of three is given the number name 'twenty-three');
5. the recording of numbers greater than ten using the number symbols (for example, twenty-three recorded as '23').

These are only the main steps. Many other points have been incorporated; for instance, the importance of 'zero' as a place-holder and the inversion of number-words in certain cases (for example, 'seven-teen' rather than 'ten-seven'). Then, of course, we have to extend the concept of place value to hundreds, thousands and so on.

Clearly we need to do plenty of work making small sets out of a number of items, appropriately recorded, before proceeding to repeated groups (wanted again later in the form of 'tables' when place value has been understood) and in particular sets of ten, probably with the names of the multiples of ten. Should we teach the twenties, thirties and forties . . . , and write these, before we write the 'teens' in number symbols so that we clear the 'rule' where the digits are written in the same order used in saying them before confusing the issue with the exceptions? The set, with various sizes of subsets, will need to be experienced with many forms of materials, as for instance, peas in cake-dishes, paperclips on rings, counters-with-holes on sticks held up in Plasticine or in cottonreels, grey pipe-cleaners held in a bundle with a red one, and so on. With the objects mentioned here a stage of abstraction can be gained when the subset is chosen of size ten, so that 10 is one full subset of ten and none over, by letting one (empty) cake-dish count for ten peas without actually filling it, or one ring count for ten paperclips without actually putting them on, one stick without its counters for ten counters, and one red pipe-cleaner represent one 'ten' of grey ones.

Similarly to move on to hundreds, seen as ten tens, the same apparatus can be extended. Ten paper cake-dishes can be represented by one foil one (or one box etc.), ten rings (of paperclips, understood) by one lace tag, ten sticks by one paste-pot, or whatever, and ten red pipe-cleaners by one blue one. The blue pipe-cleaners would already have held together ten red ones, after ten bundles of grey ones held by red ones had first been made up and then 'simplified'. These suggestions are not alternatives to the use of the more abstract Colour Factor (or Cuisenaire) rods, Dienes MAB material, or centicubes, but are recommended for use in conjunction with at least some of them. Again we can usefully ask 'Can you show these numbers with this material too? or . . . in another way? . . . or with something else?'

There are many other situations where symbolic representation can be seen as a natural extension of practical activities. Having carried out the activities by manipulating actual objects, how can we record our results? Initially young children will want to draw picutures, but if the basic number symbols and their use have been grasped then it will be seen as a natural step to represent the actions and the result using these symbols. It is then much easier to teach the conventional notation.

Visual representation and pattern

Models, pictures, diagrams, tables and patterns are needed at all levels of mathematical activity. They may help us to simplify a problem, to understand it, to represent it, to solve it or to communicate it to others. At different stages we, as mathematicians, use different forms of representation to help us recall ideas, to display them for further examination and consideration and to communicate notions effectively, more clearly and concisely or more memorably. Often abstract concepts are made more accessible by representing them in a concrete form. Young children use toys and their own 'models' to promote speech and writing, to develop vocabulary and to instigate exploration. These representations of reality provide them with the experience to develop and consolidate new skills and mental processes.

Diagrams drawn on paper are also powerful tools. They enable us to portray a situation as a whole rather than sequentially as words must necessarily do. Many diagrams enable us to use spatial means to represent non-spatial ideas, for example the number line, Venn diagrams and graphs. They can also help a child to develop mental pictures and visualizations.

Visualizations and mental diagrams have some of the characteristics of models and pictures, but we have the facility to manipulate visualizations in a way not possible with reality or models of it. However, there are dangers and we need to check what seems possible in our mental visualization against the practicalities of reality! Nevertheless visualization is potentially a powerful aid to learning and to problem-solving and needs to be nurtured in children.

What of patterns? Very young children show us quite clearly that they like regular shapes. Their early pictures are often symmetrical with people and houses drawn front-face. Patterns are also seen in many old playground games, so it is only sound common sense to use repetitions of simple shapes, actions, or numbers if we wish to enhance the children's attitude to mathematics. Pattern is at the heart of the subject and so it is appropriate to use repetition of shapes and symmetry to extract from materials a great deal of our fundamental geometrical knowledge through folding, turning, tracing and sliding, exploring tessellations and repeating a basic unit of shape in numerous ways. Some of these activities, when recorded on squared or isometric papers, have particular value in displays as new ideas 'leap out' from them.

Development of graphical ideas

The earliest graphical representation may be a concrete form of ordering, perhaps the row of beans growing in pots on the windowsill, or the ring of favourite toys sitting in a circle on the round carpet. At first these would be placed haphazardly, but they might well be rearranged, after discussion, into the order in which the owners sit in the classroom or by the alphabetical order of their names or according to their heights or, for the toys, in groups of the same type. In the last case the basic notion of a pie-chart is being established, though as yet there might not be equal spacing nor any metrical notion involved. The exercise is about sorting, ordering and comparing. However, we may decide to talk about the toys tomorrow but we want to take at least some of them home today. Thus we engender the need to make a permanent record and so each owner represents the toy by its picture. If each picture is drawn on a piece of paper of the same size, we can begin to talk about the amount of space in the ring that each group of toys needs. Thus a simple pie-chart is constructed and can be compared with a block graph representing the same situation.

There should be ample opportunity for young children to represent situations by drawing pictures of themselves or the objects under consideration. Children's natural 'feel' for fairness will soon make them want to use the same size piece of paper or 'block' to represent a single item. All kinds of 'graphs' can be constructed to represent real objects and discussed from a mathematical viewpoint. In due course they can be transferred to plain paper and, as the need for it is felt, but not before, to squared paper. The 'only thing on squared paper is a graph' syndrome must be avoided!

In the real world increasing use is being made of non-numerical as well as of numerical representations. In fact Venn diagrams, mapping diagrams, perhaps shown with bands or pins in pinboard, and networks can be used with quite young children. Tree diagrams, too, may arise naturally quite early. The possibility of using visual means to help in the growth of abstract ideas makes graphs of all kinds most acceptable both to teachers and children. It provides powerful sources of 'maths talk' and meaningful representations of relationships. Just as with reading, painting, using numbers and seeing patterns, however, development in understanding visual representation will vary in its stages from pupil to pupil. However, use of units like beads on strings, safety-pins on ribbons, pegs on ladders, names written on uniform labels can be used in group activities with each child contributing to discussion at his/her own level of understanding. While enjoying the co-operative activities, children will see mathematics as relating to everyday life and providing means of solving meaningful problems.

With the urge for longer-lasting presentations of facts we move gradually to isotype symbols or even abstract shapes mounted in groups, rows or columns, then to a coloured bar or column. We need also to remember to apply the variability principle in our use of visual representation, both by using different graphical forms for the same data and by using the same forms to demonstrate different, though perhaps similar, situations.

It is a great step, to be taken with patient understanding, when a pure 1–1 correspondence between unit squares and the objects represented gives way to a scale. Thus children are able to deal with situations where the column on a graph is no longer seen as a 'pile' of single objects. This is the first step towards representing data that is continuous rather than discrete in nature. It is an even greater step when the notion of a false origin for a scale, not starting from zero for the labelling of the axis, is introduced, and again when different scales are used on two axes.

As the complexity increases, whatever form the graph takes so too will there need to be deeper consideration of the labelling. Many early graphs may not need any label as young children know what they have done –or else they were not ready to have done it! They also love to tell anyone they can get hold of all about 'our graph', so you will have the opportunity to use the activity to develop speech, writing and reading, and to move from 'what we can say about it to each other' to 'what we need to put for someone else to know what it is about'.

When the fundamental ideas of graphical representation are appreciated the different forms possible may be used to look for logical connections, and to develop the extend ideas such as fractions, or scale and ratio. They may also assist in the formation of concepts of time and distance. Here simple flowcharts and cycle diagrams have a part to play, while scattergrams can provide a tool for use in seeking relationships and helping to develop discrimination between purely fortuitous and direct causative connections. A thorough discussion of main steps in the development of a scheme of work for pictorial representation can be found in *Mathematics 5–11: A Handbook of Suggestions* (DES, 1979).

Measurement and scale

Much is often taken for granted in dealing with measurement and scale. What does scale mean to us? Is it a little picture of a big animal, or is it a big picture of a very small animal? How can we tell? As a child grows his perception of the world changes quite quickly – from what he sees from lying down, sitting up and crawling, to suddenly standing and then continuously growing, and gaining the ability to climb on a chair, go upstairs by himself and so on. Sometimes, too, he has seen the world from Granny's knee or Daddy's shoulders, or the top of the wall, holding tightly at first to Mummy's hand and enjoying the adventure. How difficult an exercise it proves for many a five-year-old to 'find the stick that will just go in this space', even harder than finding one just as long as 'this' one. It takes some children till 6 or 7 years old to realize that physical length or weight of an object does not change with time or position. A broad object may look shorter than an equally long but narrow one and colour can also sometimes create strange effects. A child has to learn what does and what does not make a genuine difference to the (measurable) length of an object, that the largest-looking item in a collection is not necessarily the heaviest and so forth. Visual perceptions can be misleading and children need much practical experience to ensure that they do not rely on them. They have to learn the practical skills, which require physical co-ordination, and the language of measuring.

Before dealing with more advanced techniques and the introduction of standard units, they must have acquired the concepts of conservation (that an amount is unchanged by rearrangement) and transitivity (if A = B and B = C then A = C). Measurement is a very complex subject but the development of one topic area is similar to another. Hence whether learning about length or capacity a child will need to progress through direct comparison, indirect comparison, using a non-uniform, non-standard unit (such as handspan), using a uniform non-standard unit (such as Cuisenaire rod), using a standard unit, measuring by repeating a unit and using a measuring instrument. Throughout, estimation will need to be practised, the skill of approximating improved and some understanding of degrees of accuracy developed. We may consider measurement to be, as Cockcroft (1982, paragraph 269) suggests, 'a natural "way in" both to the development of number concepts and also to the application of mathematics over a very wide field'. This makes it essential that due consideration is given to developing a comprehensive programme on measurement for pupils (Shuard, 1986; DES, 1979).

Summary

In this chapter we have looked at some general issues related to children's learning. Much of the emphasis has been on the development of children's mathematics in the early stages of primary school. This has been done purposely as the needs that are beginning to be identified with infant children are the needs of all primary-age children. Thus as a co-ordinator, when devising schemes of work with your colleagues, you must give due consideration to:

1. the pupils' home backgrounds;
2. the relevance of the work to your pupils;
3. what motivates pupils to learn;
4. what is likely to make learning enjoyable;
5. the importance of developing children's increasing ability to abstract;
6. the need for practical work;
7. the importance of language, symbolism, visual representation and pattern to mathematical development.

Number, shape, pictorial representation and measurement are the fundamental elements of primary school mathematics. In this chapter we have considered certain aspects of teaching these elements to illustrate some of the underlying processes that children need if they are to function mathematically. This brings us naturally into the realms of curriculum content but it is not the aim of this book to consider content in a comprehensive or systematic way. Much of the curriculum content may be provided by commercially published textbook schemes and there are many books available to provide you with a clear structure of the development of the standard topics in a primary mathematics syllabus. A list of some of these books, together with others about language and discussion in mathematics, is given in the reference list below.

References

Cockcroft, W.H. (Chairman) (1982) *Mathematics Counts* (Report of the Committee of Inquiry), HMSO, London.

DES (1979) *Mathematics 5-11: A Handbook of Suggestions*, HMSO, London.

DES (1988) *National Curriculum, Mathematics for Ages 5 to 16*, DES and Welsh Office, London.

Shuard, H. (1986) *Primary Mathematics Today and Tomorrow*, Longman for SCDC, York.

Books on teaching approaches to primary mathematics

Biggs, E.E. and Sutton, J. (1983) *Teaching Mathematics 5 to 9*, McGraw-Hill, London.

Merrtens, R. (1987) *Teaching Primary Mathematics*, Edward Arnold, London.

Paling, D. (1982) *Teaching Mathematics in a Primary School*, Oxford University Press, Oxford.

Williams, E.M. and Shuard, H.B. (1982) *Primary Mathematics Today* (3rd edition), Longman, London.

Books on language, discussion and readability in mathematics

Brissenden, T. (1988) *Talking About Mathematics*, Basil Blackwell, Oxford.

Mathematical Association (1987) *Maths Talk*, Stanley Thorne, Cheltenham.

Pimm, D. (1987) *Speaking Mathematics*, Routledge and Kegan Paul, London.

Shuard, H. and Rothery, A. (eds) (1984) *Children Reading Mathematics*, John Murray, London.

5
CHILDREN'S NEEDS: SPECIFIC GROUPS

Introduction

The National Curriculum applies to all children and schools must provide pupils with access to it, even those with a statement of special educational needs made under the 1981 Education Act. At the time of writing it is proposed that there will be legislation making it possible to modify attainment targets and programmes of study, as well as the assessment arrangements, in special circumstances. However, this provision will not be used routinely and any disapplication of parts of the National Curriculum are likely to be temporary for all but a very few children.

To facilitate access to the National Curriculum for the estimated 20 per cent of children having special educational needs will require a careful analysis of the needs of individual pupils, a detailed study and subdivision of attainment targets and, probably, additional resources or the reallocation of existing resources, both material and human.

In this chapter we consider some of the issues that relate to the needs of specific groups of children. Dealing with these groups, however small they might be, is often seen by teachers as the most demanding aspect of their work. The very fact that these children have different problems from the 'ordinary' pupil means that teachers must spend more time devising ways of helping them. There are, of course, dangers here – notably that insufficient time will be available for the 'ordinary' child and that giving special attention to certain pupils may be seen as divisive. It is, as with most cases of classroom practice, a matter of professional judgement as to whether the balance is correct in that all children receive the appropriate amount of attention. However, a whole school policy can help you and your colleagues to cope with the pressure that dealing with certain groups of children will inevitably generate.

In an ideal world all teachers should contribute to the formulation of such policies but, even if this is not the case you as mathematics co-ordinator will be expected to advise and help colleagues with the problems. We begin by looking at general school policies relating to two important issues – multiculturalism and the needs of girls.

Multicultural (and multiracial) considerations

Any primary school needs to consider its policy with regard to multicultural and multiracial issues, and it is part of the role of the mathematics co-ordinator to ensure that these policies are implemented where appropriate within the mathematics curriculum. These policies must clearly respect and respond to the nature of the school's population. The policies needed in an inner-city school with pupils from a variety of ethnic origins must be different from those of a school with a population from a basically single ethnic background. It should not be thought that mathematics is not an important area in which pupils are introduced to some of these very important ideas. Where there are children from a variety of cultural backgrounds then the school must show that their own cultures are welcome and important to the school. This means that there must be some identification with the child's own ideas and images. Where the school is dominantly white the task of trying to give the pupils some idea and concept of the variety of people who make up our whole community, and of trying to ensure that equality and equity are principles that are developed is even more difficult.

Some of the issues are fairly clear. The texts that the school uses are likely to need supplementation by other materials designed to increase, or in some cases correct, the balance of pictorial material. Do black people always look the same? Are all the pictures obviously created with token numbers of various 'types' of pupils? Do particular children – for example, boys – dominate in doing positive actions? Recent texts are much more careful in their portrayal of roles but it is important that your pupils have an opportunity to reflect their own situation and create their own pictures. They may need to be encouraged to draw their impression of other situations too, since their own pictures may represent their own limited environment. Another important area to look at is the kind of example that the text uses. Does it use a variety of names, and not just a few stereotypes, and does it present a wide range of ideas? When discussing shopping baskets and food does it introduce a whole selection of the increasing variety now found in our stores? In the early years there may be a need to consider some mother-tongue teaching. Mathematics texts often have a fairly restricted vocabulary and parental help in translating some of them not only helps the children but gives an opportunity for parental involvement. It is possible to obtain clocks with interchangeable numbers in Punjabi or Hindi. Even with white-only classes it is not unreasonable on occasions to have a period of time when the clock-numbers might be changed, in order to give the pupils experience of recognizing not only that some cultures use different symbols, but that that is a perfectly reasonable and acceptable thing to do.

Displays and materials are another area of concern. It is important that teachers use displays in order to help 'educate' their pupils. It is obvious in a multiethnic classroom that the displays should represent the variety of pupils' cultures (does your scheme of work encourage the pupils to be involved in creating their mathematics and in personalizing the activities and displays?), but all-white classrooms should also include some displays designed deliberately to reflect the social and cultural mix of our nation. In the early years pictures used for counting activities might include a wide range of cultural objects. This could well stimulate discussion with the children of where they come from and what they do. There are some excellent sets of 'families' from different ethnic backgrounds that can be used for sorting and attribute work on mathematics (as well as in story-making).

From time to time throughout the mathematics scheme of work there should be topics specifically designed to introduce multicultural topics and issues. One particular topic which offers much of mathematical value is that of Islamic art patterns. They can be done in a variety of forms suitable for different ages of pupils and offering a range of activities to employ developing skills both in drawing and recognizing geometrical relationships and concepts.

Another topic of some value is that of shopping and food. In the early years a range of fruits, vegetables and other foodstuffs introduces the pupils to the variety of tastes and cultural backgrounds. In the later primary years the food pattern of other countries can be introduced both to give opportunities for developing general knowledge, and to introduce the idea of the need to make sensible comparisons by choosing appropriate units of measures. It is not just a question of currency exchange, but of the relative worth of a day's labour, average age and life expectation. The degree to which these issues can be tackled in detail in the primary school may be limited, but the essential ideas and concepts need to be prepared for and initiated. Television has made such topics even more important to introduce into the curriculum and very often the basis on which it can be discussed is within mathematics. Another topic often found fruitful is the consideration of world religious festivals, such as Diwali and Eid. In early mathematics they represent another opportunity to reinforce the recurrence and regularity of time. For later primary years there is the opportunity to contrast the moon-based and the sun-based calendars. There is good opportunity here for looking at number patterns.

As with all implicit ingredients in the school's mathematics it is important that the issues be kept alive and regularly considered. The multicultural mathematics curriculum must not be a static insertion into the scheme of work, but should develop and grow as teachers become increasingly more aware of what are the real issues for their school. It is the role of co-ordinators to review with their colleagues the school's scheme of work and to review the multicultural content as part of that regular consideration. It is probably usefully done once per term, either as part of the review of the maths scheme or as part of the multicultural/multiracial review. It will in the end, like most positive developments in teaching, be dependent on the attitude and awareness of colleagues. Teachers well aware of these issues will use their mathematics teaching sensitively to teach their pupils. The role of the co-ordinator is to help increase the awareness of how much mathematics can do to produce an accepting and acceptable society for the future. A list of useful articles and books is given in the appendix to this chapter, page 69.

The needs of girls

It appears to be generally true that there is little difference between the attainment of boys and girls in mathematics in the primary school. Yet there is disturbing statistical evidence that girls are seriously underachieving in mathematics. In 1985, for instance, of the passes in O-level mathematics only 44 per cent were girls and in A-level mathematics only 31.5 per cent were girls. The figure for O-level shows no significant change over previous years, but the A-level figures show some improvement over the figures in the 1970s. However, such a low percentage must still give cause for concern. Hilary Shuard (1982), in an appendix to *Mathematics Counts* (The Cockcroft Report), gives a clear picture of the differences in mathematical performance between girls and boys.

We should not, however, argue that this is a problem for the secondary schools only and that primary schools have no responsibility for this situation. The cause of this underachievement may well be traced back to early childhood. Parental expectations for girls, the sort of toys which are given to girls, the way in which they are expected to behave all contribute to an environment in which it is harder for girls to gain the experience which help one to succeed at mathematics. Boys still get Lego, and girls get dolls to play with. One is rich in mathematical ideas, the other not obviously so. The image given by the media is often of science and mathematics as male activities. More worryingly, there is a danger that computers will also be seen as belonging to the male domain. The message presented by society is all too often that boys are expected to do well at mathematics, but not girls. Mothers can be heard to console girls who have difficulties with mathematics with the idea that it does not matter and that they were no good at it either!

Primary schools cannot disregard the importance of their role in encouraging all pupils, but girls in particular need extra support to fulfil their potential. There is research evidence that teachers have different expectations for girls and boys: boys are encouraged to be experimental and adventurous, while girls are expected to be more passive. Girls are often praised for the neatness of their work, while boys are praised for the quality of their ideas. Where girls are successful, it is often by carrying out routine procedures, whereas boys succeed at topics which require a more open-ended approach. The apparent success of many girls at the primary school stage masks the fact that they are gaining success at relatively low-level skills, ones which do not prepare them well for the sort of mathematics they will meet later. This is even more of a problem in relation to the new developments in GCSE. Many of the materials used by primary schools – schemes and workcards – are sexist, showing boys being actively engaged while the girls look passively on. There is evidence that boys receive a disproportionate amount of teacher attention – probably because they tend to be noisier and more assertive.

It is essential that primary schools adopt a positive policy towards girls and mathematics. Co-ordinators have a major responsibility here. They must raise the awareness of all the teachers to the particular needs of girls, and they should see that:

1. Mathematics is not seen to be the main responsibility of the men on the staff.
2. Girls are expected to be successful at mathematics.
3. Girls are expected to succeed at problem-solving and investigative activities.
4. Girls have equal access to construction material in the classroom; make this a compulsory activity, rather than an option, for example.
5. Girls have equal access to computers, in free time as well as in the classroom.
6. Material used is non-sexist and suggests that girls too can be good at mathematics.

7. The importance of mathematics is emphasized to girls as well as boys.
8. Girls get a fair share of attention whilst working at mathematics.
9. Attention is drawn to certain advertisements, especially on TV, which stereotype the roles and expectations of men and women, and that these are discussed.
10. Parents are involved in discussion about all these issues and their own attitudes.

Children statemented as having special educational needs

As fuller integration of statemented pupils into mainstream classes looms ever larger, many primary teachers will find pupils with varying handicaps placed in their classes. Obviously the degree of handicap and mathematical capabilities of the child will vary from individual to individual but there are certain priorities that could be looked at in order to avoid some of the pitfalls previously encountered by staff.

Outside agencies

Depending on the nature of the handicap it will be possible to call on the services of the visually impaired, hearing impaired and/or physically handicapped agencies, alongside the psychological and learning support service. Their advice and special aids can prove invaluable in enabling a pupil to follow the mainstream mathematics curriculum. Small items, such as pencil grips, affixing rulers, compasses and specialist scissors can open the way for pupils with specific difficulties. Larger items, such as computer rigs, graphwriters, memowriters etc. (usually available from the physically handicapped service) can allow pupils to record their mathematics in ways other than the traditional pen/paper method.

For some physically handicapped pupils, a teacher's aide is provided. While these can be available and a most definite asset to the busy classroom, care must be taken that the pupils themselves actually undertake the mathematics and benefit from the learning process, rather than the aide doing the work for them.

Materials in the classroom

Much of the prepared work of the curriculum can be aided by the use of the duplicator. A copy of the notes can save invaluable time instead of copying from the blackboard. An enlargement of the worksheet or an extra copy to take home for parental assistance can allow the pupil to maintain the pace of the classroom and not feel stigmatized being left behind.

Above all, flexibility of approach is the key to successful teaching of the handicapped child. Preparation of lessons needs to take into account the pupil's physical limitations, but should allow for the pupil to have the satisfaction of successfully completing challenging work in mathematics.

Interaction with other pupils

Children can be both tolerant and cruel with regard to other's handicaps and the social interaction of the handicapped child can play a significant part in that child's progress in mathematics. Group work and practical work can break down many barriers, but can also create them if the same pupils always have to work together and do not wish to. Many handicapped pupils also have an emotional problem and this can sometimes hinder interaction and thus integration. Specialist advice should be sought, rather than spending teacher contact time with one pupil and forsaking the remainder of the class.

Parental/home liaison

Parents of statemented pupils can provide a very rich supply of information about capabilities, limitations and expectations. A good relationship between parent and school can maintain progress in mathematics and assist learning. Reports and reviews in mathematics should be honestly but carefully worded as all documentation related to statemented pupils is sent to parents.

Conclusion

Overall a pupil statemented as having special educational needs taught alongside mainstream pupils can be a very rewarding experience for both the teacher and the learner. If the mathematics curriculum on offer to the class is deemed worthwhile, interesting and relevant to the majority, it is only the delivery of it that may need modification for the statemented child. Allowing the child time to investigate and explore possible avenues of mathematical thought can give a rare insight into the child's capabilities and can help to ascertain true mathematical potential.

However, the extra time, thought and preparation that is made for the integration of such a pupil must be taken into account and staff involved need to discuss with each other the problems and pleasures of such teaching. This discussion needs to take place before the child moves through to another class, but also when meeting to consider the maths curriculum, its delivery and implementation. Often it is not only the pupil who needs support but also the teacher.

Extremes of ability

Only a very small number of children are statemented, but what about the some 20 per cent who have, at some time, 'special educational needs'? This term is usually applied to low-attaining and low-achieving pupils, but we must also ensure that the other end of the spectrum, the very able, receive the special attention that they undoubtedly require.

Low achievers/low attainers

What is the difference? Low achievers are those pupils who suggest, by their responses in some situations, that they are not achieving the standard of which they are capable. Basically their is a problem of motivation. They are likely to be low attainers but not because of any innate learning difficulties.

Many other children are low attainers due to cognitive disabilities. It may be appropriate to withdraw such children for specialist help. This provides the opportunity for specialist teaching of a small group or on a one-to-one basis, but the amount of time that a child is withdrawn must be thought about carefully. By withdrawing the child from the main classroom you are labelling the child as 'special'. Children who are withdrawn in this way may be deprived of many experiences that you believe are valuable and important in mathematics teaching. For instance, they might miss some of the practical experiences and group activities, and they may not have the same opportunities to discuss and to learn from their peers.

Both types of child – low attainers and low achievers – present the teacher with a considerable challenge. In some ways low achievers present a bigger problem because establishing what will motivate them can be difficult. In the case of low attainers the first necessity is to analyse carefully and in detail what is causing the blockage in their learning development. What are the prerequisite items of knowledge and experience on which the current work depends? We may have to go back several stages with the child. Most important of all we may need to present the child with the same concept but approached differently, by using different activities or different apparatus. The mathematics co-ordinator can help here by building up a stock of different types of activity, of different games and of different resources for key concepts. This will probably mean looking for new ideas in other published texts, outside of the commercial scheme used in the school.

It is important that low-attaining pupils are given the opportunity to discuss their ideas and their misunderstandings not only with the teacher but also with their peers. Other children are sometimes better than the teacher at providing the key to help a low-attaining child. If a pupil is to be encouraged to talk about his/her work the teacher must be prepared to question and to *listen* and not immediately correct the child with a dismissive 'No, that's wrong. . .'.

The very able

It is a sign of mathematically able children that they see relations quickly, understand notation easily, develop symbolism readily and apply knowledge confidently. They leap to higher orders of abstraction while the less able struggle with the lower orders. Gifted children are likely to respond better to competitiveness than their less-able peers since success has given them confidence. On the other hand they may also have over-high self-expectations. This, together with excessive parental pressures, may produce stress resulting in either severe behaviour problems or withdrawal from discussion and group activities into isolation.

It is important that such children do maintain contact with their peers if they are to develop communication skills and the ability to work with others. However, a teacher needs to keep a watchful eye on the effect that the gifted child, possessing considerable ability and achieving considerable success, has on other children in the group.

There will be some occasions, though, when special work – very different in content and style to that of the rest of the class – will need to be tackled if able children are to be extended. In such cases a teacher may feel unable to cope and it will fall to the mathematics co-ordinator to provide the appropriate material. If you feel unable to do this yourself, you could ask your local secondary school or a member of the advisory team to help.

Principles and guidelines

Whatever the abilities of individual children they will all have difficulties, albeit of varying degrees, at some time or another. There seem to be general principles that apply when planning work in mathematics whatever the level of the children.

1. Practical activities need to be provided for children, using real objects, in order:

    (a) to arouse curiosity and maintain interest;
    (b) to enable them to develop understanding and consolidate concepts;

    (c) to ensure that discussion takes place and language skills are acquired;

    (d) to allow them to demonstrate the processes they are using and to help develop symbolic representations.

2. The same concept has to be offered in an extensive variety of forms so that the similarities and differences become apparent and the underlying ideas can be abstracted.

3. Whenever possible it helps to isolate the difficulties. For example, the prerequisites can be identified and the child's understanding and knowledge of them checked.

4. Doing and talking come before recording.

5. It is important for us to use the correct language with children, allowing them to develop precision as their understanding increases.

6. Avoid teaching something that will have to be unlearned later. For example, the suggestion that addition or multiplication makes numbers and quantities bigger.

7. Be aware as far as possible of items which foreshadow important ideas to be dealt with in the future, so that *you* know how the subject develops and can teach accordingly.

8. Allow children to try things for themselves and to develop informal techniques, so that they become confident in their own ability to tackle problems.

Summary

The following list of questions may help you to focus on the main points to be considered:

1. Is there an agreed multicultural policy in mathematics?

2. Is there an agreed policy to ensure that girls succeed at mathematics?

3. Are pupils needing specialist help withdrawn from the mathematics classes?

4. If so, is this procedure appropriate?

5. What help and support is available to teachers to help them with the extremes of ability?

6. Can teachers ask for specialist help to ensure that the very-able pupils are not held back?

7. Are there supplementary materials available for teachers to use with low-attaining pupils?

8. How are all pupils given access to the National Curriculum in mathematics?

References

Mathematics education in a multicultural society

Particularly useful references

Antonouris, G. (1988) Multicultural Perspectives, *Times Educational Supplement*, 30 September.

Hemmings, R. (1980) Multi-Ethnic Mathematics: Part 1: Primary, *New Approaches to Multicultural Education*, Vol. 8, no. 3.

ILEA (1986) *Everybody Counts*, ILEA, London.

Mathematical Association (1988) *Mathematics in a Multicultural Society*, Mathematical Association, Leicester.

Maxwell, J. (1985) Hidden Messages, *Mathematics Teaching*, Vol. 111.

Zaslavski, C. (1975) African Network Patterns, *Mathematics Teaching*, Vol. 73.

Zaslavski, C. (1979) *Africa Counts*, Lawrence Hill and Co., London.

Other useful references

Antonouris, G. (1986) Multicultural: Just Checking, *Child Education*, January.

Austin, J.L. and Howson, A.G. (1979) Language and mathematical education, *Educational Stages in Mathematics*, Vol. 10.

Bourgoin, J. (1973) *Arabic Geometric Pattern and Design*, Dover, New York.

Bourgoin, J. (1977) *Islamic Patterns*, Dover, New York.

Brown, T. (1987) Issues in 'multi-ethnic' education, *Mathematics Teaching*, Vol. 120.

Dawe, L.C.S. (1983) Bilingualism and mathematical reasoning in English as a second-language, *Educational Stages in Mathematics*, Vol. 14.

Emblem, V. (1986) Asian children in schools, *Mathematics in School*, Vol. 15, no. 5; Vol. 16, no.1.

Fasheh, M. (1982) Mathematics: culture and authority, *For the Learning of Mathematics*, Vol. 3, no. 2.

Grugnetti, L. (1979) School mathematics makes Sardinians healthier, *Mathematics in School*, Vol. 8, no. 5.

Head, J. (1918) Personality and the learning of mathematics, *Educational Stages in Mathematics*, Vol. 12.

Hemmings, R. (1984) Mathematics, in Craft, A. and Bardell, G. (eds) *Curriculum Opportunities in a Multicultural Society*, Paul Chapman, London.

Hudson, B. (1987) Multicultural mathematics, *Mathematics in School*, Vol. 16, no. 4.

Jones, P.L. (1982) Learning mathematics in a second language: a problem with more and less, *Educational Stages in Mathematics*, Vol. 13.

Joseph, G.G. (1984) The multicultural dimension, *Times Educational Supplement*, 5 October.

Joseph, G.G. (1987) Foundations of eurocentrism in mathematics, *Race and Class*, 28.

Mitchelmore, M.C. (1980) Three-dimensional geometric drawing in three cultures, *Educational Stages in Mathematics*, Vol. 11.

Northam, J. (1982) Girls and boys in primary mathematics books, *Education*, Vol. 10, no. 1.

Tahta, D. (1987) Islamic patterns, *Mathematics Teaching*, Vol. 119.

Woodrow, D. (1984) Some cultural impacts on children learning mathematics, *Mathematics in School*, Vol. 13, no. 5.

Girls and mathematics

Burton, L. (ed.) (1986) *Girls into Maths Can Go*, Holt, Rinehart and Winston, London.

Hughes, P. (1988) Buried bias, *Times Educational Supplement*, 30 September.

Open University/ILEA (1986) *Girls into Mathematics* (PM645) Cambridge University Press, Cambridge.

Shuard, H. (1982) Differences in mathematical performance between girls and boys (Appendix 2), in Cockcroft, W.H. (Chairman) *Mathematics Counts*, HMSO, London.

Walden, R. and Walkerdine, V. (1982) *Girls and Mathematics: The Early Years*, Bedford Way Paper 8, University of London Institute of Education.

Walden, R. and Walkerdine, V. (1985) *Girls and Mathematics: From Primary to Secondary Schooling*, Bedford Way Paper 24, University of London Institute of Education.

6
THE PRIMARY
MATHEMATICS CURRICULUM

Introduction

The introduction of the National Curriculum might lead you to believe that there is no longer any need for you to consider the mathematics curriculum. This is to misunderstand the National Curriculum documents. As we mentioned in Chapter 1 the National Curriculum prescribes two distinct but complementary items, namely attainment targets and programmes of study. Programmes of study are given for each level, and hence each key stage, and have the appearance of syllabuses. Indeed the programmes of study are said to be 'the essential content which needs to be covered to enable pupils to reach or surpass the attainment targets . . . . They are the basis on which teachers will develop schemes of work to implement the curriculum in maths' (National Curriculum Council, 1988, paragraph 6.1). Thus the programmes of study provide the *framework* for the curriculum, rather than the complete curriculum itself.

You and your colleagues will need to plan the approach, select the activities, organize the environment and choose the teaching styles which go to make up the curriculum.

In order to help you carry out these tasks we start this chapter by considering some of the general theory that is currently seen as appropriate in the analysis of curricula. You will need to use the insights gained from a study of this theory to help you analyse what is happening in your school.

The curriculum

During the past decade much has been said and written about the school curriculum. Since the word 'curriculum' can mean different things to different people, it may prove useful to begin by discussing how the word will be interpreted within the present context.

The following views are contained in *The Curriculum from 5 to 16* (DES, 1985):

> A school's curriculum consists of all those activities designed or encouraged within its organizational framework to promote the intellectual, personal, social and physical development of its pupils. It includes not only the formal programme of lessons, but also the 'informal' programme of so-called extracurricular activities as well as all those features which produce the school's 'ethos', such as the quality of relationships, the concern for equality of opportunity, the values exemplified in the way the school sets about its task and the way in which it is organized and managed. Teaching and learning styles strongly influence the curriculum and in practice they cannot be separated from it. Since pupils learn from all those things, it needs to be ensured that all are consistent in supporting the school's intentions.

This definition of what comprises the school curriculum is broader than that which some people would espouse, yet in a sense even this is perhaps too narrow. As well as all the learning experiences which a school provides deliberately, children learn a lot in incidental and unintended ways. Sometimes this learning is very positive and constructive: children may develop their own ideas and strategies for coping with mathematics in a way which increases their confidence and flexibility. Unfortunately much incidental learning can be very negative: in mathematics lessons children can easily develop poor self-esteem and an unhappy relationship between the teacher and themselves.

Aims of the curriculum

When making decisions relating to which and what type of activities should be included within the school curriculum, teachers, parents and educationalists are often guided by statements of educational aims. Aims proposed in *The School Curriculum* (DES, 1981) include:

> – to help pupils to develop lively, enquiring minds, the ability to question and argue rationally and to apply themselves to tasks and physical skills;
> – to help pupils to acquire knowledge and skills relevant to adult life and employment in a fast changing world;
> – to help pupils to use language and number effectively.

The curriculum needs to be designed to ensure that all pupils are prepared to meet the common basic intellectual and social demands of adult life, but it must also contribute to pupils' present wellbeing as well as to their ability to develop to the full their individual potentialities. The apparently conflicting demands of present and future, common and individual needs, can create great tensions when making decisions relating to which activities should be included in the school curriculum.

Broadly speaking our aims in mathematics education are:

1. To develop mathematical skills and understanding within the pupil's capabilities.
2. To develop the children's abilities to apply mathematics to real and novel situations.
3. To encourage children to work systematically independently and co-operatively.
4. To encourage a positive attitude to mathematics and an appreciation of its intrinsic fascination and value.

A major task of the mathematics co-ordinator is to translate these broad aims into learning objectives in mathematics.

Objectives in the mathematics curriculum

A lot of different classifications of objectives in mathematics have been produced, but the basic list is much the same (Cockcroft, 1982):

1. facts;
2. skills;
3. conceptual structures;
4. general strategies for problem-solving and investigation;
5. appreciation of the nature of mathematics and attitudes towards mathematics.

Facts

There is a small body of knowledge in mathematics which is sufficiently useful to be worth knowing by heart. This is not to say that such knowledge is properly or effectively learnt by rote, indeed in most cases we have acquired immediate recall of such facts by regular usage in meaningful situations.

As an example, ask yourself 'What is 7×5?' Your immediate response is not to think 'What does is mean?' or 'What do I have to do?' but '35'.

Now compare your reaction to 7 + 5. For most people the response 12 is just as automatic as the 35. Yet few of us learnt both these facts through the same kind of process.

Figure 6.1

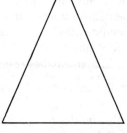

What is the special name for a triangle like this (Fig. 6.1) which has two equal sides? Can you identify what made you think of the answer to this question? Was it the words 'two equal sides' or the stimulus provided by the picture of the triangle? The interesting lesson from this example is that the answer is provoked by different stimuli for different people.

Factual information is believed to be most effectively learnt in interesting and relevant contexts which enable pupils to realize its significance and importance. If facts are to be memorized, this is easier after patterns, relations and rules have been perceived and understood.

Skills

Skills are procedures that you learn how to perform. You may be taught standard step-by-step instructions for some skills, or you may invent your own method which you then apply time and again in the same way. Traditionally primary mathematics has been dominated by the teaching and learning of particular algorithms – step-by-step routines for doing arithmetic using pencil and paper. In practice we do need some procedure for finding the answer to calculations we do not remember the answer to. To test yourself, try subtracting 25 from 112. What did you do? Surely you did not begin by saying '5 from 2, I cannot take'. Furthermore, if you were given a calculation well beyond your powers of mental arithmetic you would most likely reach for a calculator. Both the pencil and paper method and the calculator are devices which allow us to stop thinking about the meaning of the question and produce the answer by a mechanical process. In this sense they have comparable validity but both, in their time, have been the most effective method of obtaining the solution.

Despite the amount of time given to pencil and paper arithmetic in primary schools, most people never became very proficient in this and made little use of the skills in everyday life. Technological change means that such skills are redundant, and the ability to use a calculator sensibly and with understanding has replaced them. Such evidence as there is about children using calculators suggests that the effects are entirely positive, and fears that proficiency in mental arithmetic would suffer have proved unfounded.

There remain many performance skills which are important in learning mathematics, measurement skills and reading of scales and dials are of particular significance.

There is reason to believe that skills such as these are best acquired in the course of activities which appear worthwhile in themselves to both pupils and teachers, and that the contexts in which a skill is acquired should enable pupils to apply and practise the skill as well as to master it.

Conceptual structures

If facts are things that you remember and skills are things that you perform, then conceptual structures are things that you recognize and understand. This understanding demands a recognition of properties and relationships. An example of this kind is found in APU's *Mathematical Development: Primary Survey No. 1* (Assessment of Performance Unit, 1980) (Fig 6.2).

Figure 6.2

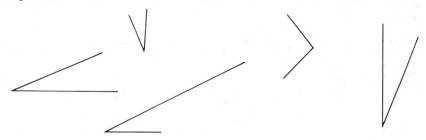

Which of these angles is different in size from all the others? This question demands the abstraction of one particular feature, the size of the angle, from a variety of features and distractions in the situation. A comparable kind of task can be produced to show depth of understanding of the place value conceptual structure; for example, put these in order of size:

357   753   357   735   537   573

Work in schools should be practical; it should be directly concerned with 'making and doing'. In primary schools pupils need to handle water, clay, paper and constructional toys in order to acquire and develop concepts and skills. As they progress through their schooling their practical experiences should continue and expand to include experiences of working with a broader range of materials, designing, experimenting, planning and testing. Moreover, work which is not directly concerned with making and doing can be based upon practical activity and real experience. Concrete experiences form the basis for abstract thinking.

General strategies for problem-solving and investigation

Traditionally, when a mathematics curriculum is described it is common practice to list only the facts and skills that are to be taught. In recent years attempts have been made to identify the concepts to be acquired. These three – facts, skills, concepts – comprise the *content*.

Even more recently, attention has been given to the identification of strategies which promote problem-solving and investigation. General strategies, which form a part of the range of *processes* involved in doing mathematics are difficult to describe, but it is important to try to describe them so that they are not overlooked in curriculum building.

We need to try to provide a range of activities which will encourage children to invent their own strategies for solving problems. Think about this task (Fig. 6.3).

Figure 6.3

How can you cut up two squares and rearrange the pieces to make one single square?

It is possible to have the knowledge, skill and understanding required of this task, even to the extent of recognizing whether an answer is right or not, and yet still be unable to complete it. The problem demands a certain amount of creativity; it demands that you invent something for yourself, it demands a certain kind of insight.

Abilities of this kind can be developed. The fashion for the problem-solving and investigational work in primary mathematics education is very much concerned with providing the appropriate experiences for such development.

Appreciation of the nature of
and attitudes towards mathematics

Appreciation is concerned with what kind of activity mathematics is and what it is for. You might believe that mathematics is a set of arbitrary rules which you learn in order to pass tests. Or you might believe that it is an interesting and creative activity that can provide satisfaction and fulfilment. Or again, you might think of it as a useful set of tools and techniques that help you to cope with the reality of everyday life. All of these contain some truth, but each contains its own value judgement and we need to consider carefully what sort of view of mathematics we wish children to acquire (see Chapter 2 for a fuller discussion of this).

Attitudes can be considered to be overt expressions of personal values which may arise in a variety of particular situations: attitudes may not be fixed, they may vary according to circumstances. For example, pupils who are generally favourably disposed towards school may have a negative attitude towards a particular subject area because they do not perceive its relevance, or because they achieve little success in that particular area.

In the APU surveys attitudes are tested by pupils' responses to certain statements which enable us to identify attitudes on a number of scales. Thus we ask whether pupils believe mathematics to be easy or hard, whether they like or dislike the subject, or whether they believe it is useful or relevant. If pupils are allowed to express their feelings about learning mathematics in more open ways other features emerge more prominently. Good and bad emotional responses are usually associated either with the level of pupil esteem within the classroom or on the perceived relationships between pupils and teachers. In these circumstances styles of teaching and classroom organization probably have a more significant effect on children's emotional response than the nature and content of the mathematics concerned.

A model for the primary mathematics curriculum

How do these elements fit together to form the mathematics curriculum? We have said that facts, skills and concepts form the *content*. Shuard (1986) suggests that general strategies form part of the set of *processes* (see Chapter 2) that make up mathematics. *Appreciation and attitudes* form another element. Also children learn mathematics in a particular *situation*, usually through an experience or activity devised by the teacher. Hence Shuard derives a model with four aspects that she represents by the four faces of a tetrahedron (Fig. 6.4).

Figure 6.4

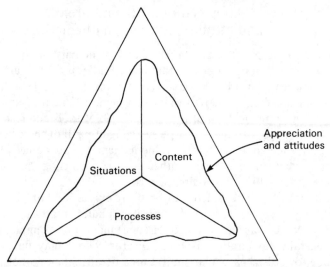

Clearly this is still only the core of the curriculum and there are various other factors which influence the way in which the curriculum is delivered and the way in which it is perceived by the pupils. In the rest of this chapter we look at some of these factors.

Classroom organization

Within all schools there are generally accepted organizational arrangements. In a primary school, each teacher is allocated her own class with whom she normally spends most of her time in her own classroom. Within these generally accepted arrangements many organizational alternatives present themselves. There will be times, such as when a class project of a thematic nature is being launched, when pupils in the class will benefit from feeling that they are members of a single corporate body. During these class sessions the teacher will need to exercise a wider range of skills; for example, she will need to be particularly careful to ensure that the material selected will be accessible to all pupils (at their own level) and to ensure that all pupils are able to see, hear and contribute.

At other times, pupils will benefit from working in small groups: when pupils work as a group on a common task they need to co-operate, to exchange views, to share ideas and resources. Sometimes, the pupils in each group will benefit from being with others of similar interests and ability, but on other occasions a group of mixed ability and interest can be more profitable. Careful thought needs to be given to the composition of groups as different types of tasks are undertaken. Very different educational outcomes result from different ways of grouping and it is a matter for individual professional decision-making as to which is the most appropriate form of grouping for each particular activity.

Any system which encourages children to take any responsibility for their own learning depends for its success on making the children as independent of the teacher as possible.

See that as much basic information is readily displayed in the room. Opinions might differ as to what should be there, but it would probably include a large number-line, tables of relationships between measures, diagrams to show that a right angle has 90 degrees, the spelling of difficult words like parallel, isosceles and so on.

Make sure that children know where everything is kept, and establish the fact that everything has to be replaced after use.

Make sure that children know what to do when they need help – that they look round the room, use reference materials, look at a mathematics dictionary, ask another child . . . and, in the last resort, ask you!

There will also be times when pupils need to work individually, for example, each pupil needs to be able to read, write and do mathematics himself/herself.

In essence, flexibility of grouping and group size is to be recommended. When making decisions about how groups should be formed it is helpful to consider the aims and objectives of each task: would these be achieved more effectively in groups of similar ability or interest? It may also be useful to explain to pupils what is happening and why you feel they might benefit from certain types of grouping; they can then organize themselves within the constraints the teacher feels are appropriate:

1. general instructions may be to the whole class;
2. explanation may involve groups or individuals;
3. discussion is most effective in small groups;
4. practical work may involve a group or an individual.

Teaching and learning styles

Traditional teaching methods rely heavily upon exposition by the teacher followed by consolidation and practice by pupils. Knowledge is transmitted from 'knower' to 'learners' and then each 'learner' performs tasks to consolidate or practise what has been learned. Within this model of the learning process each pupil works as an individual member of a class.

Recent moves towards more active forms of learning which place emphasis on practical work, investigational approaches and problem-solving create opportunities for pupils to work co-operatively as members of a group and to exchange views and ideas as they discuss details of their collective tasks.

Some teachers find the management and organization of group work difficult because they lack experience of working in this way. Success when using these less traditional teaching strategies is based upon good relationships. Children need to believe that what they do and say is of value to their peers as well as to their teacher and they need to feel that their ideas will be sympathetically received.

Children need to be encouraged to work together successfully in a group. Take care over the way the tables and chairs are arranged. It is impossible to work well as a group if the children cannot all see each other. They need to sit round a table so that no one is left out of the discussion.

Think about the grouping of the children, and the balance between their ability to get on well together and also of their ability to work at much the same rate.

It is also important that pupils should be clear about what is expected of them and that there should be well-established classroom routines and practices. Features of effective group work often include:

1. a preliminary exchange of ideas and views between teacher and pupils based on previous experiences, together with materials that are available and can be handled, read, looked at from a variety of angles, smelt etc.
2. clear task definition, including a statement of time available for completion of the task, together with the provision of an appropriate amount of resource materials needed;
3. division of the class into groups in which each member of each group has a clearly defined role, for example, scribe, spokesperson, recorder, etc.
4. reporting back to the whole class of the agreed findings of the group through the spokesperson;
5. class discussion of the main findings of the groups, which may be chaired by a pupil or the teacher;
6. exhibition of work produced.

Organizing discussion with the whole class

If the idea of discussion in mathematics is to be encouraged, we need to think how to manage the classroom environment to make it more likely to happen.

Allow plenty of time for pupils to contribute. Try to tolerate pauses or even quite long silences and not to rush in to fill all the gaps. It is hard to restrain ourselves – we often answer our own questions before the pupils have even had time to absorb the question. Allow them both thinking and answering time.

Encourage children to listen to each other. Often children are keen to talk to the teacher but are rather intolerant of each other's contribution. Techniques such as asking the other children what they think of another's comment can help. 'What do you think about what Jill has just said?' 'Do you agree with that?' 'Can you add to that idea?' And so on.

Discourage children from interrupting – either when you or they are talking. There needs to be some accepted way of indicating that you want to say something – preferably not by yelling out or even wild waving of hands!

Organizing group discussion

When children are working in groups a teacher's role in intervening in the discussion can serve many purposes. The following classroom discussion checklist taken from *The Language of Functions and Graphs* (JMB/Shell Centre for Mathematical Education, 1986) provides a useful summary.

During classroom discussions, a teacher's role should:

1. mainly be that of a 'chairperson' or 'facilitator' who:

   (a) directs the flow of the discussion and gives everyone a chance to participate;
   (b) does not interrupt or allow others to interrupt the speaker;
   (c) values everyone's opinion and does not push his or her own point of view;
   (d) helps pupils to clarify their own ideas in their own terms;

2. occasionally be that of a 'questioner' or 'provoker' who:

   (a) introduces a new idea when the discussion is flagging;
   (b) follows up a point of view;
   (c) plays devil's advocate;
   (d) focuses in on an important concept;
   (e) avoids asking 'multiple', 'leading', 'rhetorical' or 'closed' questions that only require monosyllabic answers.

However, pupil talk and group discussion should be valued without it being necessary for any orchestration or intervention on the part of the teacher.

Barnes (1976) states:

Pupils' talk is important in that it is a major means by which learners explore the relationship between what they already know and new observations and interpretations which they meet.

It may well be that if children choose their own discussion groups the talk may be freer and the results will be more fruitful than if the groups are chosen by the teacher.

The impact of technology

Computers

The new technology is now a fact of pupils' lives at home, if not yet in school. In their use of new technology many pupils are in advance of most of their teachers. Even if pupils only use their home computers for playing arcade games, they know how it works, within this limited context, and they are not afraid of it.

Almost every primary school in Britain now has at least one computer, and most primary school children have some experience of using the computer at school.

Almost all of the use of computers in primary mathematics involves the use of published software. The value of this software is enormously variable. Some programs are designed to provide individual pupils with practice and consolidation of skills previously acquired. This is a wasteful use of scarce and expensive resources. Some programs are designed to support *problem-solving* and *investigation*; they can be particularly useful to teachers and pupils who have little experience of these activities. Good software can be used to stimulate *discussion* and can be effective when used either with a whole class or with small groups.

Ideally the use of the computer should be seen as an integrated part of classroom activity; the computer is an aid to teaching and learning just as is a blackboard or squared paper. In many circumstances the work on the computer will be the first stimulus for much classroom activity.

One of the more unfortunate aspects of early teaching programs was that the computer told the children what to do. A significant criterion in evaluating software could be the amount of control and choice it gives to children. For this reason there is some considerable value in programming activities. Any kind of mechanism which allows children to write instructions and set up procedures for the computer to follow is worth considering. LOGO does exactly this, and those who would like to think more carefully about the principles upon which this is based can read Seymour Papert's (1980) book, *Mindstorms*. Seen in this context LOGO has two great advantages: it allows children to control the computer; and it provides a wealth of opportunity for investigational work, not only in geometrical situations but also in number and language. For a lot of good general information about using computers in teaching mathematics read Ball (1986).

Calculators

The use of a calculator for learning mathematics is now well documented. One of the most important areas of concern may well be how to convince your colleagues and parents that the use of calculators as a commonly accepted resource alongside all other apparatus is appropriate in learning mathematics.

Some teachers have begun to explore with their classes the calculator's potential for providing a more exploratory approach to mathematical ideas and have faced new questions. They now see the calculator as an integral part of their number curriculum and have been forced to reconsider the way they might use a commercial scheme and other packaged material.

What might happen when a calculator is used as a resource to investigational enquiry?

1. It could help to demonstrate how much challenge and fun there is in thinking mathemetically.
2. It could help to show that learning mathematics is more than just doing 'sums'.
3. It could help to show the children that their own invented methods are worthy of discussion and debate and that the sharing involved can help to further their thinking.
4. The children meet such mathematical ideas as negative numbers, large numbers and square root much earlier than is usual and many children appear to able to make some 'sense' of these notions.

These are just some of the statements offered by teachers who have tried this approach – there are obviously others that could be added.

Clearly the calculator might influence how and what the pupils learn. The following list suggests some of the attitudes and approaches that integrating the use of calculators into the mathematics curriculum could affect. As the mathematics co-ordinator you will need to think about all these possibilities and encourage the use of the calculator to promote good practice in your school.

The use of calculators might:

1. increase *motivation* (positive attitudes to maths);
2. generate *discussion* – child/child and child/teacher;

3. generate *enthusiasm* for mathematics – children *and* teachers!
4. help build confidence;
5. enable attention to focus on *problem-solving*;
6. act as a *catalyst* for new mathematics learning;
7. give opportunities for '*trial and improve*';
8. enable pupils to work with realistic numbers;
9. be a useful *diagnostic* aid;
10. reinforce *concepts*, such as place value.

Some thoughts on teaching and learning mathematics

For all pupils the learning of mathematics can be an enjoyable, sometimes exciting, experience. But this will only happen if learning to think mathematically becomes our aim rather than the acquisition of an eclectic collection of facts, skills and concepts.

Mathematics is not merely a body of knowledge which can be transmitted from teacher to learner. It is a way of interpreting our environment through which we can problem-solve and make predictions.

Using the language of mathematics we can produce mathematical models of everyday life situations; using mathematical skills we can perform operations within mathematical systems to obtain solutions to our mathematical problems. These mathematical solutions can then be interpreted to give us answers to our real-world problems.

Pupils will not find it easy to function in this way if their teachers view mathematics as 'knowledge to be transmitted'. Mathematical problem-solving must be the driving force. The acquisition of knowledge which can be used for interpretation and for problem-solving requires fundamental changes in teaching strategy.

Pupils need to be allowed to experiment, using practical materials. They need to understand that mathematical symbols enable us to produce a model of the real-life situation. The rules that must be observed when manipulating the symbols must be understood. Finally, reinterpreting the answer to the real-life situation requires not only translation skills but judgement.

Such ways of thinking are not acquired through the passive assimilation of predigested knowledge: they require active participation by the pupil. Practical experience is, however, not sufficient; pupil–pupil discussion which enables the learner to see things from perspectives other than his own and encourages reflection upon the shared experiences ensures that each pupil organizes and reformulates his own knowledge for himself. This is the type of knowledge that promotes understanding and enables the learner to become an active problem-solver, not only able to answer questions but also able to ask them.

If we want children to see mathematics as an activity in which creativity and imagination are important, then our classroom environment needs to reflect this. We need to encourage questions such as 'What would happen if . . . ?', 'I wonder if . . . ?', 'What if . . . ?'

Make sure that there are always a range of different mathematical activities in the classroom. If you use a published textbook scheme, see that it is also supported by some investigative starting points, games, puzzles, problems to solve and so on. There are plenty of resources for ideas available now.

See that *you* also are seen to be using these 'enquiry' type questions. In other words, that there can be activities in the classroom in which you are genuinely interested, and that you do not already know everything there is to be known about them!

Above all, present mathematics, not as a mysterious 'black box' of which some 'clever' people know the contents, but as an activity that has to be investigated, in which trial and error, good guesses and 'I wonder if' and 'how can I find out?' are the really important attributes.

The role of assessment

As is suggested in *A View of the Curriculum* (DES, 1980):

> The curriculum has to satisfy two seemingly contrary requirements. On the one hand it has to reflect the broad aims of education which hold good for all children, whatever their capabilities and whatever the schools they attend. On the other hand it has to allow for individual differences in the abilities and other characteristics of children, even of the same age . . . . If it is to be effective, the school curriculum must allow for differences.

Sensitive observation by the teacher is an essential first stage when making appropriate provision for each individual pupil's needs. Some pupils learn more quickly than others; some pupils work more effectively in small, homogeneous groupings; some prefer to work with particular pupils who may not be of similar ability. For all pupils the teaching strategy used is a crucial factor; some may always find it essential to be able to handle concrete objects, while other pupils rapidly move on to more abstract forms of reasoning and require quite different types of intellectual challenge.

It is important that teachers should provide learning experiences which ensure that each individual child makes progress across the curriculum. However, this progression will not take place at a uniform rate. Some individualized learning, workcard-based approaches facilitate rapid progression through skills to be acquired at the expense of the development of concepts and problem-solving skills. If children are to develop and build systematically upon their existing range of knowledge, concepts, skills and attitudes a well-ordered selection of teaching and learning experiences must be planned, and the rate at which pupils are invited to move through this programme of activities is a matter of professional judgement.

Assessment, be it formal or informal, is inseparable from the process of teaching. Whenever we engage in an activity it is natural for us to form some judgement relating to how well it went or how it was received. Teaching is a goal-centred activity; we teach in order that our pupils may learn and our yardstick is graduated accordingly. After pupils have completed a learning task, it is natural for a teacher to question what pupils have learned. Did the pupils acquire the intended knowledge, skills, concepts? Did they solve the problem posed? If not, why not? Were the objectives appropriate? Were the teaching strategies suitable? How should the approach be modified next time?

Questions such as these can only be answered when there has been a clear definition of expected outcomes. While some outcomes are easily assessed because pupils may have used pencil and paper, many are more nebulous and difficult to assess; they require discussion with individual pupils rather than the marking of written work. There are also outcomes that can only be assessed after a lengthy period of time.

Much assessment takes place informally within a busy classroom and is largely impressionistic. Even in such cases it is useful if teachers communicate their assessments to pupils. If there has been clear task definition, at an appropriate level, pupils respond well to discussion of the strengths and weaknesses of their efforts. This can occur quite naturally during teacher–pupil verbal interaction.

From time to time more formal assessment may take place. Whenever possible, assessment tasks should be constructed so that they provide valuable learning experiences and a basis for future action.

A fuller discussion of assessment procedures can be found in Chapter 10.

Summary

A curriculum is not a syllabus nor even a programme of study. In mathematics the curriculum is dependent upon the types of activity and experience, because these enrich and extend the essential content, and upon the teaching and learning styles, because these enable the content to be delivered in a meaningful and effective way.

As mathematics co-ordinator you will need to consider various aspects of the mathematics curriculum in your school:

1. the aims of the curriculum;

2. the objectives in terms of:
   (a) facts, skills and concepts;
   (b) processes;
   (c) attitudes;

3. the teaching and learning styles in terms of:
   (a) activities;
   (b) problem-solving;
   (c) investigations;

4. the use of technology:
   (a) calculators;
   (b) computers;

5. classroom organization for:
   (a) the whole class;
   (b) group work;
   (c) individual work;
   (d) discussion;

6. the role of assessment.

References

Assessment of Performance Unit (1980) *Mathematical Development: Primary Survey Report, No. 1*, HMSO, London.

Ball, D. (1986) *Microcomputers in Maths Teaching*, Hutchinson Educational, London.

Barnes, D. (1976) *From Communication to Curriculum*, Penguin, Harmondsworth.

Cockcroft, W.H. (Chairman) (1982) *Mathematics Counts* (Report of the Committee of Inquiry), HMSO, London.

DES (1980) *A View of the Curriculum*, HMSO, London.

DES (1981) *The School Curriculum*, HMSO, London.

DES (1985) *The Curriculum from 5 to 16*, HMSO, London.

JMB/Shell Centre for Mathematical Education (1986) *The Language of Functions and Graphs*, JMB/Shell Centre, London.

National Curriculum Council (1988) *Mathematics in the National Curriculum*, NCC, London.

Papert, S. (1980) *Mindstorms: Children, Computers and Powerful Ideas*, Harvester, Cambridge.

Shuard, H. (1986) *Primary Mathematics Today and Tomorrow*, Longman, London.

7
RESOURCES

Introduction

The maintenance of a stock of material resources for teaching mathematics is an obvious responsibility of the subject co-ordinator in a primary school. This chapter discusses the general issues you will need to consider when providing resources for mathematics teaching, while Chapter 9 looks at the more specific tasks you will have to undertake in order to manage these resources effectively. Although a most important aspect of your work, organizing and maintaining resources is probably the most thankless. At the beginning it can seem overwhelming – and you will find few willing volunteers to help you sort through old cupboards to tidy up or classify the stock. In accepting responsibility for resources, you need to come to terms with three issues.

1. You are not starting from scratch, either with the materials available or with the teaching staff.
2. Many of your resources are not specifically designated for mathematics but are available for any curriculum activity.
3. Whatever you decide you *want* financial limitations will determine what you can *have*. Let us consider these issues one at a time.

Existing resources

Very occasionally a new primary school opens and one person has *carte blanche* to set up mathematics resources. You may dream of this opportunity, but the chances of it coming your way are virtually nil. Most likely, you have been designated as the person with responsibility for mathematics in a school where you have already been teaching for a short while. Alternatively, you may have accepted, more or less willingly, a special post for mathematics in another school. While these are different situations, it may not be this difference so much as your own personal style and your opinion of the existing provision within the school which determines how you proceed.

The idea of a new broom sweeping clean is one that newly appointed staff usually consider and almost immediately reject. Most people want to see the existing system ticking over for a little while before suggesting radical change. In the management of resource materials, however, it will not be very long before you become frustrated by the cautious, sensitive, softly-softly approach. The trouble is that you want to know just what is available in the school, and to feel that, in co-operation with colleagues, you have some control over it all. To acquire this knowledge and power, you may well feel you need to go through everything; and some schools contain a surprisingly large accumulation of material. Probably within about a year of taking up your post, you are ready to carry out a full-scale blitz on the mathematics resources. This blitz is emotionally difficult. For a start you will be reluctant to throw anything away, and other people will be even more reluctant to let you. Amongst those boxes of old worksheets there may be the inspiration for a wonderful lesson. That old, hand-operated calculator that has been jammed for years might be a good aid for work on place-value, if you spent a bit of time getting it going again! But be ruthless. You have neither the time nor the storage space for self-indulgence. If you like, you can set out all your unwanted rubbish in boxes for staff, pupils and passing strangers to pick up like jackdaws. If you want to avoid this spectacle, then choose your time and means of disposal carefully.

Of course, your blitz on resources is not a secret operation, and you do not have absolute authority to dispose of assets at will. Many teachers tell stories of expensive equipment which has proved virtually useless yet been kept for years because no-one has the courage or the authority to throw it away. Some local authorities circulate an 'exchange and mart' newsletter, through which you may be able to get rid of items you do not want and acquire equipment which you need. If the school possesses a great deal of old material, this may be a worthwhile opportunity to discuss matters with an LEA mathematics adviser or some other knowledgeable person from outside the school, who can look at what there is and take a more detached view of it all. In a very old-established school, you may find old textbooks or even examples of children's work that are of historical interest and value; it is worth getting advice about such material.

Shared resources

Most resources used in teaching mathematics are not specifically dedicated to that purpose but are available for many aspects of the curriculum. This is obviously true of staff and of classroom accommodation, but it also applies to nearly all materials. Ordinary items such as paper, card, scissors and pencils are used for all kinds of activity, and so are sophisticated devices such as video-recorders and microcomputers. Even more specialized items such as maps, weighing scales and tape-measures might seem more relevant to geography or science than to maths. There may be a small amount of special equipment including, perhaps, Unifix blocks and abacuses; but almost everything you use is general property rather than mathematical stock.

Having particular responsibility for mathematics, you may find this sharing of resources a little untidy, but it is worth reflecting on why it is like this. First, mathematical activity is not something which happens only in mathematics lessons, it is a part of the way we think and behave in many situations. This is why materials that promote and develop such activity are often to be found and used, not only in other school subjects, but in everyday life. Most teachers would be happy to encourage this view and avoid the tight separation of school mathematics into its own compartment.

Second, and perhaps more realistically, the control of resources reflects the internal structure of a primary school. You are not a head of department in the way that a senior mathematics teacher may be in a secondary school. Especially in more traditional secondary schools, departments are likely to maintain their stock and be funded as separate sections. In a primary school, if resources are not held centrally, they are just as likely to be allocated to year groups or to class teachers as to subject specialists. You need to be aware of how materials are ordered and controlled in your particular school, and it might be useful to you to try to classify the resources available according to how these are held. For example, the headings might be:

1. items held centrally and available for all classes and subjects (microcomputer, video-recorder, etc.);
2. material kept by class teacher in classroom, base or area (paper, card, textbooks or workcards for particular group, etc.);
3. resources for teaching mathematics available for any teacher or class (enrichment material, books of mathematical activities, computer software, etc.).

Of course, the appropriate classification will vary according to the organization within the school.

It is worth saying that the benefits of sharing resources are personal and professional as well as curricular. Occupational isolation is a familiar hazard of teaching and, whatever the attractions of having your own subject, your own class, your own room and your own cupboard, this leads not only to a wastage of resources but to a loss of co-operative effort. Conversely, the need to share materials can lead to a sharing of ideas and expertise.

Financial limitations

Most people would like to feel that educational provision has moved on from the emphasis on collecting cartons and other household rubbish and producing home-made apparatus out of nothing. The technological developments of the 1970s and 1980s mean that children are accustomed to sophisticated, professional presentation of materials. However, a lot of this entertainment, especially the dominance of television, places children in an inactive, and frequently solitary role. Thankfully, the personal involvement and social activity of the primary classroom remains an important and central influence in children's lives. While we are not trying to compete, as teachers, with the compelling entertainment standards of the media, we do have some responsibility to provide learning tools for children which are as attractive and contemporary as the devices they are used to seeing outside school.

Resources cost money, and no-one would seriously advocate financial stringency as educationally beneficial. On the other hand, during the 1960s and early 1970s, there were examples of profligate waste in education. It is now more generally accepted that conservationist and environmental considerations require a careful use of many consumable materials, and an ordinary concern for other needs within the community means that we cannot always demand a major share of resources for our own particular interest. It is important to distinguish, however, between this caring realism and the kind of short-term economy which allows equipment and buildings to deteriorate beyond repair through lack of maintenance. While these matters may not be your immediate concern, they can determine the financial climate in which you have to work.

At some stage, especially if you have the kind of blitz suggested, you will feel the need to make an informal audit of available resources. It is useful if you can make a list both for your own use and for the information of other staff. With this background, you will begin to recognize the main needs and deficiencies; and, in the context of each year's budget limits, you will be able to decide on your priorities.

Workcards and textbooks

The development of a mathematics scheme for a primary school is discussed in Chapter 8. From a resource point of view, the main issues concern the nature and amount of material to be provided, the way in which it is stored, and how effectively it is used. The first consideration, however, may be whether and when to change the existing scheme.

Most primary schools have a set of books, workcards or other, usually published, materials on which the teaching of mathematics is more or less faithfully based. Is it going to be necessary to change it? Unless the scheme has been recently and perceptively chosen, and given that you expect to have responsibility for mathematics for a few years at least, the answer is likely to be 'yes'. Historically, it seems that the final part of the twentieth century is a time for rethinking the objectives, relevance and value of school. The recent introduction of a National Curriculum is the culmination of considerable review and analysis of mathematics teaching over the past 7–8 years. One result may be that your current scheme does not fulfil adequately the demands of the National Curriculum. For instance, a scheme that fails to introduce pupils to the use of calculators may be seen as inadequate and will need to be either replaced or at least supplemented.

Schemes that include only sets of textbooks are currently less fashionable than those that rely on a combination of materials including workcards, worksheets or small booklets; and, where textbooks are used, they are usually confined to the upper end of the primary age-range. Even in middle schools that bridge the traditional division between primary and secondary age groups, schemes using textbooks alone are less popular. While large collections of workcards and the like are more flexible and sometimes more economical than books, their use demands carefully thought-out storage and diligent record-keeping.

Because needs vary so much amongst schools, it is unlikely that any published scheme will satisfy you exactly. This has tempted some schools to produce their own schemes, with teachers writing and reproducing all the material (see Chapter 8). This exercise, while apparently attractive, is an enormous, labour-intensive undertaking and may well not be the best way of using teachers' time. The sensible and selective use of a published scheme, with additional enrichment material is frequently more efficient. In the same way, it is sometimes possible to readapt an old, existing scheme, using some parts and replacing others to meet changing needs and ideas in the school. The extent to which this is an economical proposition, compared with adopting a new scheme, is again a matter for careful judgement.

Equipment

Large technological aids such as televisions, video-recorders and audio tape-recorders, microcomputers, and film and slide projectors are normally centrally stored and belong to the whole school rather than to a particular class or specific curriculum area. It is often more convenient to have these items on trolleys so that they can be moved to different class areas when required, rather than shepherding groups of children to another part of the school to use the equipment.

While taking stock of this equipment, it is worth considering which members of staff feel able to cope with using it. There is a tradition in some schools that only one or two teachers can set up technical aids, while others develop a learned helplessness about using them! Looked at objectively, this is a ludicrous situation. Most equipment found in schools demands very little physical strength, dexterity or intelligence to operate it. The more staff who feel confident with such apparatus, the more imaginative and effective use will be made of it.

One of the more difficult aspects of resources work is the maintenance of a stock of relevant, up-to-date software, so that technological aids can be used to best effect. You need to be particularly aware of new videotapes and computer disks and to discuss these with other staff, so that everyone knows that they are available.

Most small items of equipment and stationery need to be available in the classroom where they are to be used. Catalogues of educational suppliers will give you more than enough ideas of what is obtainable. Indeed you will have to tailor your demands according to the money and space allowed to you. Card and various kinds of printed paper are especially useful. It will often be found more economical to buy the largest size sheets available and cut these to the required size.

Calculators

In the discussion of resources, calculators need special consideration, both because they are an important resource in themselves, and because they raise questions about the provision of resources that have implications for all kinds of items that children are expected to have and use at school.

The importance of calculators as a resource has itself two aspects. First, the sensible use of calculators for everyday arithmetic must become part of the curriculum. As the National Curriculum documents make clear, it is no use ignoring calculators or pretending they are peripheral to the serious business of pencil and paper arithmetic.

Second, there are many aspects of mathematical competence where calculators are a valuable aid to teaching and learning. In practical work, they enable children to work with real data and measurements without the calculations becoming impossibly laborious and investigations of series and number patterns can be carried out quickly and easily. Estimates can be checked immediately, and in many situations feedback to the pupil is direct and non-threatening.

It is one thing to become convinced of the importance of calculators in primary mathematics, but how are they to be provided? In one sense, the ideal arrangement is for children to own their own calculators, and use them regularly both in and out of school. The familiarity, personal control and independence associated with this probably outweighs any argument about the cost or about the great variety of calculators which will appear. On the other hand, some teachers prefer to have a set of calculators for class use, and certainly some spare ones will need to be available.

In most schools, the cost is not a serious consideration. Simple calculators are much cheaper than a lot of other things which children are expected to take to school. The kind or model of calculator to be provided is a more difficult issue. Even if you suggest that children buy calculators, you may well want to make a recommendation about this. Some have argued that you may as well buy a calculator with a lot of facilities, claiming that children are well able to ignore the buttons that are not needed. Most children are, but those who keep pestering you to explain what the buttons are for can be a distraction. One manufacturer has even produced a mask to fit over a calculator, covering up items that are not likely to be used in primary school. This is all somewhat unnecessary. The best solution is probably to have a calculator with just $+$, $-$, $\div$, $\times$ functions and, preferably, a square root. We are not buying something to use for a lifetime, and more sophisticated devices are going to become cheaper in future years.

There are basically two types of calculator available: arithmetic and scientific. The simpler, cheaper calculators are usually arithmetic calculators; these will give the answer 20 to the question $2 + 3 \times 4 =$. The calculator performs the operations in the order in which they are entered. If you are ordering calculators for your school these are perfectly adequate for primary school children. However, you and your colleagues need to be aware that if children bring their own calculators some of these may well be scientific calculators. Scientific calculators will give the answer 14 to $2 + 3 \times 4 =$. Here the calculator performs the operations according to standard functional priority (for example, multiplication has priority over addition) as if the question were $2 + (3 \times 4) =$. It is not a problem that calculators function in different ways as the children can learn a lot from exploring the different or similar behaviours of their calculator.

Calculators with rechargeable batteries can be obtained, but these are not such an asset now that longer life batteries are readily available. Solar-powered calculators are both common and cheap and are the most simple and convenient to use in a primary school classroom.

Microcomputers as a resource

The widespread availability of microcomputers in children's homes and in the outside world is perhaps itself an argument for having these devices in schools. It is possible to argue for some kind of computer awareness courses even at primary school level. But that is not the immediate concern here. We have to consider the microcomputer as a resource for teaching mathematics. In this respect its role will inevitably change and develop, but it seems possible to identify a number of distinct ways in which microcomputers are at present used in primary mathematics.

A large number of programs are designed so that the computer is used as a teaching machine. Many of these provide little more than repetitive practice of skills and are of no obvious value. In fact, much of the work would be better done through worksheets! Programs for teaching specific skills can sometimes be useful if they are used as part of a package with a variety of teaching approaches. There are, for example, some good programs on mapwork that have associated maps, worksheets or other material provided with them.

A number of recently developed programs have taken the form of adventure games, with a variable amount of mathematical activity. Good software of this type is now readily available. You will need to look at the kind of activity involved, its appropriateness for the children's age and ability, and its appeal, particularly in the use of graphics. It is hard to predict, however, what features are likely to make a game compelling so that children will want to keep working on it.

Some programs allow you to do nothing more than load and run them. This may seem like a waste of the computer facility but good animated geometrical film sequences are now being produced in this way. A lot of discussion and creative mathematical activity can be generated in the classroom from such a stimulus.

During the years in which home microcomputers have been popular toys, those children who have them seem to have used them in only two major ways: to play arcade games and to write programs. There has always been scepticism about the value of programming in BASIC for primary children, but it is clear that most children are capable of programming in LOGO.

Teachers with an interest in mathematics are often especially enthusiastic about the use of LOGO. There is no doubt that work on LOGO can develop a wealth of understanding and provide a rich context for investigative work in geometry. Hopefully, experience over the years will provide some guidance as to how these developments may best be exploited in the classroom.

In general the most worthwhile uses of the microcomputer in primary mathematics education is to be found in using software that gives the children a fair degree of control over what they are doing. While using this type of software the children can make and test hypotheses. There is a fair amount of good software available and it is your role to discover and acquire this software. Your teachers' centre will usually be very helpful in both having examples of the software available, and in knowing what software your LEA has bought licences for, and therefore what you can freely copy and what you need to buy.

Reprographics

All schools have some facility for duplicating items such as letters to parents, handouts and worksheets for children. Sometimes these arrangements are limited, but in many schools there is the choice of photocopier, stencil printer or 'Banda' style duplicator. The extent to which these are used will depend on several factors: the adequacy of the published scheme used in the school, the cost of reproducing materials and the amount of time and effort teachers are willing to give to the production of their own material.

It is worth giving a little thought to how worksheets in particular should be produced. Many teachers would justify the use of a simple Banda handout for a particular lesson because it is quick and cheap to produce. On the other hand, if the material is to be used more generally, a more professional-looking document may be more appropriate, probably typed rather than handwritten. A 'Jumbo' typeface is useful for worksheets for younger children. There is a trend in some schools to set very strict standards about handouts and worksheets, particularly if these are to be seen outside the school. This has some validity when parents' perceptions of school standards are based on the pieces of paper that children collect.

If extensive use is made of handouts and loose sheets of paper, care needs to be taken over the way in which these are kept. If children build up collections of sheets including some work of their own, these can easily become very scrappy in appearance. Careful and meticulous use of folders and files is needed in this situation.

Some teachers are a little shy and even perhaps possessive about their own worksheets. This is a shame. As in many other matters, there is a lot to be achieved by the sharing of ideas, resources and work. If a teacher produces good material, then others will benefit from seeing it and sometimes using it; and, if some staff are unhappy about some aspects of the work that their colleagues are giving to the children, then there is a need to provide a chance for them to say so tactfully and discuss it openly. The organization of this will depend upon professional relationships within the school but, as an ideal, it is worth trying to make available to everyone copies of all handouts and worksheets used.

Television and radio programmes

Both BBC and ITV produce TV series on mathematics for primary children. Usually there is a book of teacher's notes and sometimes a pupil's workbook to supplement the TV programmes. A series is usually reshown each year for 2 or 3 years and then replaced. Details of the programmes are likely to be sent direct to your school, so keep an eye open for the introduction of a new series. A programme is usually repeated either the same week or the following week. Some rescheduling or a break in the series in mid-term caters for different half-term arrangements. Even with this choice it may not be feasible, nor indeed desirable, for your classes to watch the programmes at the times of transmission; so you may have to arrange to record them.

As mathematics co-ordinator you should take responsibility for informing colleagues what programmes are being transmitted. You will have to send off for the teacher's notes and any pupil materials (or purchase them from an educational bookseller). In addition, you may have to help with arrangements for booking the TV or for ensuring that the programme is recorded.

TV programmes can set up situations, use cartoons and graphics, and visit places that it is impossible for you to provide, produce or arrange. Their visual impact, therefore, can be considerable. However, they do need to be used carefully. First, you must be sure that the level is appropriate for your pupils. Second, you must prepare. You must know the content of the programme, what it is attempting to do and which concepts, skills and techniques are involved. Usually there is little value in just letting your pupils watch the programme. It may be necessary to set up some introductory activities and it will certainly be necessary to follow up the programme with discussion and supplementary or extension work. Third, the programmes often cover a lot of ground in a short period of time, so there is not the necessary time for consolidation and practice. To provide this, be prepared to use only part of a programme at any one time, leaving other parts for another day. *Knowing* the programmes is vital, therefore, if you are to ensure that they are used as effectively as possible.

BBC radio also transmits, or produces on cassette, some mathematics programmes. Most of the points about TV programmes apply when using these.

Accommodation

The designation of a particular room in a primary school as the specialist mathematics room is neither practicable nor advisable. Some years ago, for a short time, the idea of a mathematics laboratory was fashionable in some quarters, but the accepted view is that mathematics is part of the ordinary class activity and needs to be catered for within the classroom, base or area. The particular accommodation of mathematics equipment depends very much upon the type and design of the school – for example, is it open-plan, semi open-plan, classroom-based? Is it family-grouped or year-based? This topic is dealt with in more detail in Chapter 9.

Displays

A display can involve material obtained commercially or produced by the teacher, set out in the classroom to provide a stimulus or for a specific teaching purpose. It can also be, particularly with group and individual work, an opportunity for children's work to be shown to, and shared by, the rest of the class – or even the whole school. Provision has to be made for such displays on the wall, on special display screens and stands, or on tables. The best displays are confined to areas designed for the purpose, where they serve real purposes and are not just ways of covering up drab walls.

Displays should not stay as they are for very long. Children soon learn to accept them as part of the landscape, and the element of stimulation disappears. Material other than children's work should be chosen either to act as a focus for a particular lesson or to stimulate some activity; and when it has served its purpose (or failed to do so) it should be changed. There are a very few exceptions when numbers or multiplication tables or specific information may need to be permanently on display.

In most primary classrooms, much of the display area is likely to be taken up with children's work. Here again it may be better to change this often. The work soon loses its fresh appearance after a few days on the classroom wall. Probably a small amount of work on exhibition changed frequently is better (and easier to look at) than a vast and congested wall-to-wall display. When arranging for displays of children's work, remember to consider three-dimensional materials such as geometrical models.

Some displays are really activity areas. In this category come classroom shops or banks or areas with a display of mathematical games or puzzles. A particular activity area of this sort can be especially useful as children can go and become involved in the work, while at the same time the area provides a semi-permanent focus of visual interest.

Books and journals

As well as the books and materials which make up the teaching scheme, there is a place in primary mathematics for a variety of other publications, either to provide enrichment materials for the pupils or to keep staff informed of curriculum developments in mathematics education.

Books which provide useful enrichment material include some on the history of number, some concerned with geometrical pattern, design and models, and a wide range of publications containing puzzles, problems and games. If there is a school library, you will want to ensure that a reasonable selection of books about mathematics is included. It is easy to recognize that children's libraries everywhere have a strong bias towards certain subject areas, but not usually mathematics!

It is of course important that teachers in the school are aware of books which can be used to provide interesting material for lessons and group or individual work in mathematics. But there is another category of books which should be available to teachers: those which encourage continuous reconsideration of the content of the curriculum and of approaches to teaching mathematics. This category includes any recent DES reports and HMI discussion documents, as well as reports and guidelines produced by the local authority. You will find it useful, either as an individual or as a school, to become a member of the Mathematical Association and the Association of Teachers of Mathematics. Both associations publish journals and reports which give insight into teaching mathematics at primary level.

People as a resource

Several sections of this chapter contain hints and suggestions that the most effective use of resources depends on discussion among colleagues. The sharing of ideas by the teachers concerned is an even more crucial aspect of this than the sharing of material resources, and a forum needs to be provided in which this sharing can take place in a relaxed but constructive way. The wealth of ideas, enthusiasm and experience amongst the staff of a school is a resource which is easily underexploited. Discussions need to be seen not just as a means of support for less confident staff, but as a way of picking everyone's brains; and it needs to be accepted that all teachers can benefit from the exercise.

Links with people outside the school can also be a source of fresh ideas. Your most obviously useful contact may well be with a local authority adviser, but contacts in other places, for example, a nearby teacher-training institution, are worth developing. It is a good idea – some would say essential – to arrange some kind of working link with one or more of the mathematics staff in the secondary school to which your pupils transfer. In some places, there are well-established working parties involving the staff of a secondary school and its feeder primary schools. If you are fortunate enough to have a teachers' centre, and particularly a specialist mathematics centre in your area, then this is a place to which you should naturally go to meet other people, for advice, and to look at equipment.

In-service development

Like the strength and expertise of staff, in-service opportunities are not always regarded as resources, but they are a facility available to teachers, who can choose whether and to what extent they make use of the opportunities.

There is a view that, for many teachers, the most useful in-service work takes place in the classroom and is directly related to their own teaching. It can certainly be valuable if you are able to arrange this in school. Short courses can be very exciting, but they take teachers out of the classroom for the initial stimulus and then leave them to their own devices. Some kind of follow-up work is usually necessary. In other respects, the pattern of in-service training for teachers has developed and changed considerably over the years and is likely to go on doing so. Directed days can certainly be used to very good effect. Longer courses, more advanced courses, and courses involving an element of retraining have to change all the time to meet the demands of teachers and the needs of the education service.

Courses intended to train primary teachers to give leadership in mathematics have existed for some time, and by far the commonest such course is the Mathematical Association Diploma in Mathematics Education. This course is usually run on a part-time basis. In some places, in-service BEd or BPhil(Ed) courses have included substantial consideration of mathematics education at primary school level. These courses have served the dual purpose of enabling experienced teachers to update their certificate qualification and develop expertise in an important area of the curriculum. Obviously, such a course has a limited market, and in areas where it has been established for a few years that market may have been exhausted. Diploma courses and in-service BEd courses have probably both suffered from recent rationalizations of teacher-training institutions, which have left some areas of the country with very little provision of this nature.

More academic in-service courses exist in most universities and a number of other higher education institutions. Many master's degrees in education can include courses in mathematical education; again such degrees are usually taken by part-time study. Opportunities are also being arranged for teachers to spend a term or more out of their own classroom, either as 'teacher fellows' in higher education or working within their local authority. These can be valuable opportunities to identify, develop and evaluate good classroom practice.

Summary

The maintenance of resources is a major responsibility of the mathematics co-ordinator. You need to consider:

1. What are the existing resources?
2. Which materials are general resources used also in other parts of the curriculum?
3. Which materials need to be stored centrally?
4. What are the financial implications of providing and maintaining resources?

You must take responsibility for a wide range of resources and facilities, including:

1. equipment (some of a general nature as well as that specifically mathematical);
2. reprographics;
3. workcards;
4. textbooks;
5. calculators;
6. microcomputers;
7. TV and radio programmes;
8. accommodation;
9. displays;
10. books and journals.

Don't forget that *people* (from both inside and outside your school) provide a valuable resource. There is more about this, and about in-service training, in Chapter 9.

8
THE MATHEMATICS SCHEME

Introduction

The development of a mathematics scheme has already been discussed briefly in Chapter 7 on resources. In most primary schools the scheme is the central resource for teaching mathematics. It forms the essential framework on to which activities and materials are built. Chapter 7 considered, in passing, the possibility of a school producing its own complete scheme. This can be a very rewarding task but it requires confidence, expertise and an enormous time investment from teachers.

Even if you do not intend to produce a completely school-devised scheme, it is worth discussing with colleagues the *idea* of devising a scheme. First, the exercise will be useful in giving you some idea of what aspects of your existing provision you want to keep. If you want to make changes, buying a complete package from a publisher is not the only option and is certainly not a complete answer to your needs. It is more than likely that you and your colleagues will want to retain and to develop a number of activities which you feel are valuable to your children. It might be sensible to consider whether you could produce a framework or an outline mathematics curriculum in which these activities might be incorporated. Second, discussing the production of your own scheme, even if you subsequently reject the idea, will give you a lot of insight into the things you want to look for in published material.

One of the problems with starting to look at commercially produced schemes is that you and your colleagues immediately begin picking out features which you particularly like or dislike. There is an obvious temptation to make these features into criteria for adopting or rejecting the material. Yet in a sense this is the wrong way round. You really need to try to establish what you want from a scheme before examining what is available. The Mathematical Association (1986) has published a set of discussion papers, *Choosing a Primary School Mathematics Textbook or Scheme*, and this package includes a considerable amount of analysis which teachers might carry out *before* any scheme is scrutinized. Lumb (1984) also provides a checklist to help you choose a published scheme. An alternative approach, however, is to begin by deciding what you would want in a scheme produced by and for the school.

The programmes of study given in *Mathematics in the National Curriculum* (DES, 1989) provide a framework, in terms of content, for the scheme. However, it must be realized that there remains considerable freedom in *how* the content is delivered. In particular, the choice of learning experiences, the range of teaching approaches and the type of classroom organization is still the responsibility of the school and of individual teachers. Only general guidance is given by the National Curriculum Council.

The mathematics scheme in the primary curriculum

In constructing a mathematics scheme, especially at primary school level, few would want to divorce their planning considerations from the general work of the school. Schools vary enormously in their approach to mathematics teaching, and there is a sense in which this reflects something of the aims and values of the school and its staff. This is true of academic objectives, but it is even more applicable to personal skills and values. It is useful to set out some guiding principles which characterize your school's approach; otherwise, there is a danger that concentration on content considerations may lead to the production of materials that teachers are unhappy to use.

We suggest here a number of questions which you might ask, grouped under various headings.

Children's freedom and responsibility

1. Do we want to provide detailed instructions about how and when each piece of work should be done, and how it should be recorded?
2. Do we want to encourage children to plan and organize their own work, and to express it and set it out in their own way?
3. What is the right balance between these?

Providing for a range of aptitudes and interests

1. How are lessons going to be organized?
2. Do we want opportunities to talk and work with the whole class, together on one activity?
3. Do we want materials that encourage or require the children to work in small groups?
4. How much of the scheme is going to require children to work as individuals?
5. Do we want a substantial core of material on which all the children will work, with perhaps some enrichment activities for more able children and remedial activities for those who experience difficulties?
6. Or do we want a broad variety of materials on each topic with a range of difficulty, so that we can provide quite different activities for children of different aptitudes or interests?
7. Is there some way of providing an appropriate balance between these two extremes?

Recognizing different aspects of learning

1. How important is it that children should know some facts by recall?
2. How important is it that children should be able to perform certain standard skills?
3. How important is the recognition and awareness of mathematical relationships and structures?
4. How important is it that children should devise their own strategies for solving problems?
5. How important is the children's emotional and affective response to mathematics?
6. What relative weight do we attach to each of these different aspects?

Issues of social class, race and gender

1. How do we want the scheme to reflect differences of class, race and gender?

The role, style and autonomy of teachers

1. What role will individual teachers have?
2. Will teachers be prepared or competent to accept resonsibility for adapting and using the material in their own classes?

3. Do your colleagues want very detailed guidelines for classroom activity in mathematics?
4. Or, would they prefer to develop more of their own ideas and extend the material as they go along?
5. How much specialist knowledge and expertise in mathematics do the teachers have, or want to develop?

Assessment and record-keeping

1. Is there a clear policy on assessment in the school or in the LEA, and does it meet the requirements of national testing?
2. Does the mathematics scheme have to fit into, or allow for any specific forms of assessment and evaluation?
3. What kind of records do you need to keep, and how should the scheme cater for these?

The school curriculum in a broader context

1. What is the relationship between you and the mathematics department of any secondary school to which your children transfer?
2. Do you have understanding or expectations of what each other is doing?
3. Does this in any way affect your mathematics scheme?
4. If there are separate infant and junior schools, how is the mathematics provision co-ordinated?
5. How will your scheme meet the national requirements for the school curriculum?

These questions are just as valid, whether you are producing your own materials or choosing a commercially available scheme. In either case, you will want to discuss these issues with colleagues and probably with people outside the school, including an LEA adviser. You can then develop general guidelines within which mathematics teaching in the school has to be accommodated. It seems sensible to do this *before* you start producing materials, or you look at published schemes, and even before deciding which of these alternatives is right for you.

The content of the scheme

The criteria discussed so far have been concerned both with the way in which mathematics is taught and learned, and with the kind of learning which you think desirable. No doubt you will feel the need to develop more detailed criteria for mathematical content. By and large, however, content is a relatively simpler area in which to make adjustments. Indeed, as already mentioned, the essential content is provided by the programmes of study in the National Curriculum documents.

You may feel, when comparing your scheme with these programmes of study, that some aspect of mathematics is neglected or overemphasized in your scheme. To resolve these differences it should be fairly easy to introduce some new material or to spend less time on certain topics, as appropriate. This is quite different from discovering that the scheme demands styles of teaching and organization which do not fit into your school; problems of this nature are likely to prove far more intractable.

There may well be some aspect of the school's work in mathematics which is well developed, and liked by both teachers and pupils. This may have become a particular strength in the school curriculum, it may give a special flavour to your work, and you may feel able to take a pride in this. If you can identify activity of this nature, and it helps pupils to achieve a particular attainment target or set of targets, then you will obviously want to incorporate it in your new scheme. Clearly you do not need to look for this particular work in a published scheme – you already have the resources and expertise and you can use the topic to enrich the published material.

On the other hand, there will clearly be some aspects of mathematical activity that you feel need introducing or strengthening. This might include, for example, starting points for investigation and problem-solving, or activities to develop the sensible use of calculators, or some work with microcomputers. Identify these areas. If you are producing a scheme, you may well decide that you need books and other published material to provide certain particular ideas and expertise. If there are activities that need greater emphasis in the school, and a published scheme does not provide for this, then you will have to produce or look for suitable enrichment material. You may find it difficult to produce your own investigations but this is not true of all topics. If, for example, you feel it necessary to provide more practice in mental arithmetic and a scheme does not explicitly include this, you will probably find it relatively easy to produce some appropriate materials.

A detailed analysis of the mathematical content of the different primary mathematics schemes can be found in *Maths Links 1 and 2* (Turnbull, 1981/1987). The discussion papers by the Mathematical Association (1986), already mentioned, also include extensive tables and checklists for analysing the mathematical content of published schemes.

However, it is probably important not to become over-anxious about the fine details of subject matter. Children who acquire positive attitudes to mathematics, who become confident in their own ability to devise strategies for solving problems, and who learn to handle numbers and mathematical relationships in their own way are building a firm foundation for future mathematical development. Children learn skills and negotiate ideas in many different ways, often using procedures quite unlike those they have been taught. *Mathematics for Ages 5 to 16* (DES, 1988) stresses that levels within attainment targets 'should be achievable as a result of good classroom practice', and the importance of the quality of the experience and the flexibility of thinking must not be underrated.

Maybe the most crucial part of mathematical subject content is the linguistic aspect. You will no doubt want your pupils to become familiar with a range of words and symbols commonly used in mathematics. Can you say what these are, and do you expect the scheme to introduce and use them? At the same time the ordinary language in a scheme, and for that matter its layout and presentation, are critical factors in its acceptability to pupils and teachers. If you are still thinking of producing your own scheme, you will no doubt pay careful attention to these features. If by now you have decided to look for a published scheme, make a note of these language and presentation considerations, before you start looking.

The social and cultural context of the scheme

One of the questions that we suggested you might ask about a mathematics scheme is how it should reflect differences of class, race and gender. On the whole, teachers have become more aware of, and sensitive to such issues in recent years; and it is unlikely that anything obviously offensive or disparaging to one section of the community would escape your notice or be acceptable. On the other hand, material presented to children can contain hidden messages, sometimes of a subtle kind, of which we need to be aware. You may find the ILEA (1986) publication *Everyone Counts*, useful in helping you to identify instances of this.

Like any other form of teaching and learning, mathematics education can be used to advertise and support particular prejudices and views of the world. There are situations in which some may feel it justifiable to use teaching in this way; but, whatever our ethical opinions on this, it is important to realize what we are doing, and not to let propaganda creep in by default.

In practice, of course, if mathematics is about anything real, it cannot be culture-free or value-free. Whatever decision we make about the proportion of male and female characters in our scheme, for example, and in whatever role we cast these characters, that decision carries with it some message about our view of the world – either as it is, or as we should like it to be. Of the matters under consideration here, perhaps the gender issue is the most obvious. The portrayal of men and women in material for children, and the acquired disadvantage of girls in mathematics education in later years are separate but linked concerns. We need to show men and women in reasonably equal numbers in a variety of roles, not allocated according to gender stereotypes. At the same time, the contexts and situations in which we set illustrations of mathematical tasks and structures need to be extremely varied, to reflect the range of interests and experiences of children, regardless of whether these interests may be associated conventionally with one sex rather than the other.

It is increasingly accepted as well that schemes and texts should reflect the varied ethnic origins of children in Britain. This means including pictures of children from different racial groups and using names other than traditional English ones, but this is a somewhat superficial recognition of cultural differences. At best, it would be worthwhile to value and recognize sensitively the variety of social activity, belief and lifestyle which a mixture of cultural groups can provide. Perhaps it is asking a lot to expect a mathematics scheme to incorporate this idea, but it is important to be attentive to the principle.

There are many other ways in which schemes can suggest the superiority of certain categories of children. Children may be presented as clean, middle-class, healthy, well-dressed, and having money to spend. All may appear to have two parents, and the text may reflect a family structure which is thought desirable – though hardly typical. Ask yourself whether you want the scheme to show children wearing glasses or with disabilities or just looking sad or scruffy.

One effect of media advertising is that we become accustomed to people being presented as glamorous. We are provided with a conventional notion of what is physically attractive, and there is a temptation for pictures in schemes to imitate this. After all, the publishers want the scheme to look attractive and to sell well. Yet are these really the features that we wish to promote as desirable?

In the end, no scheme will entirely satisfy you in this respect. You will be left feeling uneasy with something in any scheme you adopt because of some image or bias or stereotype that it includes. Perhaps the sensible approach is to accept that this is part of any material and to point this out to your pupils. You can discuss what you feel is wrong about the presentation, and even ask why it is like this.

How to choose a scheme

Let us suppose that you have gone through the exercise as suggested. You have asked questions about the place and style of mathematics learning within your school; you have looked at the subject content and compared it with the programmes of study given by the National Curriculum; and you have given some thoughts to cultural considerations. This analysis may have led you to decide that producing your own scheme is probably not the best way for your school. Now you want to find out about some published schemes. How do you go about it? As a device for choosing a scheme, the Mathematical Association discussion papers are worth attention. They provide you with a very thorough procedure, and even if you feel this approach is over-elaborate you will be able to select some useful techniques. Lumb (1984) also produced a booklet to help you 'critically appraise' a published scheme. The appendix to this chapter contains a document to help you analyse the strengths and weaknesses of a scheme and to assess its suitability for your situation.

However, these papers do not refer to particular schemes and, as has already been explained, publications which do analyse schemes rapidly become outdated. How then do you find out about the published textbook schemes?

It is not difficult to obtain superficial information from publishers as publicity material is readily available, and advertisements appear in journals. Very detailed knowledge, however, is a little more difficult to come by. Publishers will generally supply you with sample packs, but may be reluctant to let you have a complete scheme on loan or approval. Nevertheless, you should try to get as much as you can and it is to be hoped that publishers may be persuaded to allow more extensive inspection facilities.

Your local authority may have a collection of schemes. If you are lucky, you may be able to find these at a teachers' centre or resource centre. A nearby teacher-training institution may have material which you can look at. Best of all, of course, is the opportunity to evaluate schemes in use and it is certainly useful to visit other schools to see material that you might consider adopting.

Cost will inevitably be part of your deliberations. It would be very sad, however, to allow this to become the main consideration, overriding educational criteria. Try to decide first what you would really like and then look at the cost to decide how you can afford it. It may be possible to justify relatively large expenditure because of the comprehensive way in which a scheme provides for your needs. Material that appears less costly may prove to be a false economy. You may find yourself purchasing lots of enrichment material, apparatus and all kinds of consumable materials.

In financial terms, you have three matters to consider:

1. the total cost of equipping the school with the scheme (and any additional resources needed);
2. how this is going to be spread over time if the scheme is to be phased in;
3. what sort of recurrent expenditure your school may be committed to in the future.

Currently available schemes

Within the foreseeable future, there is not likely to be a shortage of published schemes to choose from! There are many primary schools, all of them teach mathematics, and changes in emphasis generate a continued demand for new schemes. This is a potentially lucrative market for publishers.

Sometimes, for a little while, one scheme appears to become dominant, but even this can vary from one part of the country to another. In some areas in the late 1960s, *Alpha* and *Beta* books were to be found in most schools. During the 1970s, a lot of schools adopted 'Fletcher' maths (the common name for *Mathematics for Schools*). In the mid-1980s, advertisements claimed the Scottish Primary Mathematics Group (SPMG) scheme to be 'the most widely used maths scheme in UK primary schools'. There is no adequate survey of the current situation, and the predominance of a particular scheme or series is a remarkably fleeting phenomenon.

As well as advertisements, the journals *Mathematics Teaching* and *Mathematics in School* regularly contain reviews of schemes, and articles about their content and use. A general framework for choosing a scheme is given in an article by Harling (1979) in *Mathematics in School*. The same author with Tessa Roberts (1988) has produced a comprehensive list of criteria for analysing a mathematics scheme. Some articles look at very specific aspects: for example, Pamela Liebeck (1985) has compared the treatment of length in various schemes in an article in *Mathematics Teaching*. New schemes are usually reviewed in some detail, but *Mathematics Teaching* (1984), no. 108 contains brief reviews of half a dozen schemes.

Once the scheme is chosen, you will need to introduce it into your school. In Chapter 9 you will find some comments about the different possible ways of doing this.

Supplementing your scheme

No published scheme of work is perfect and you will soon discover the need for supplementary materials. We are very fortunate in this country that we have a wealth of interesting supplementary materials in mathematics readily available. Indeed some schools reject the wholesale adoption of a particular scheme in favour of a school-produced structure, supported by a collection of books, resources and computer software.

You will need to work through any supplementary materials that you think may be suitable and develop ideas about how they might be presented to children. In this way many exciting ideas for investigative and problem-solving activities, in particular, can be discovered and distinctive, innovative work can be developed.

Summary

The introduction of a National Curriculum may lead teachers to believe, at least initially, that the mathematics scheme has been prescribed. This is far from the truth as the choice of activities, the styles of teaching approach and the type of classroom organization will still be the responsibility of individual teachers.

The key issue still confronting the mathematics co-ordinator is whether to construct your own scheme or whether to buy in a commercially produced scheme. In order to reach a decision on this you will have to carry out detailed discussions with your colleagues and consider, in particular:

1. children's freedom and responsibility;
2. the range of aptitudes and interests of your children;
3. the different aspects of the learning process;
4. social class, race and gender issues;
5. the role, style and autonomy of teachers;
6. methods of assessment and record-keeping;
7. the relationship between the mathematics curriculum and the primary curriculum as a whole.

The content of the scheme will have to satisfy the programmes of study of the mathematics National Curriculum.

If you choose to adopt a commercially produced scheme you will need to obtain as much information about the available schemes as possible and be prepared to supplement your chosen scheme with other materials.

References

DES (1988) *National Curriculum, Mathematics for Ages 5 to 16*, DES/Welsh Office, London.

DES (1989) *Mathematics in the National Curriculum*, DES and Welsh Office, London.

Harling, P. (1979) Choosing texts for primary school mathematics, *Mathematics in School*, Vol. 8, no. 4, September.

Harling, P. and Roberts, T. (1988) *Primary Mathematics Schemes*, Hodder and Stoughton, Sevenoaks.

ILEA (1986) *Everyone Counts: Looking for bias and insensitivity in primary mathematics materials*, ILEA Learning Resources Branch, London.

Liebeck, P. (1985) Early Steps in Measurement, *Mathematics Teaching*, no. 112, September.

Lumb, D. (ed) (1984) *Primary Mathematics: Critical Appraisal Instrument*, Longman for Schools Council, York.

Mathematical Association (1986) *Choosing a Primary School Mathematics Textbook or Scheme*, The Mathematical Association, Leicester.

Mathematics Teaching, no. 108, Book Reviews (September 1984).

National Curriculum Council (1988) *Mathematics in the National Curriculum* (Consultation Report), NCC, York.

Turnbull, J. (1981/87) *Maths Links 1 and 2*, NARE Publications, Stafford.

APPENDIX: LOOKING AT A
PUBLISHED PRIMARY MATHEMATICS SCHEME

Description

1. Range of materials available:

   (a) Textbooks/workbooks/worksheets/workcards
   (b) Topic books/extension materials/reinforcement materials
   (c) Teacher's manuals/investigational material/assessment materials/computer software.
2. What additional resources are needed?
3. Modes of use: individual/group work/whole class.
4. Are the rationale and aims clearly defined?
5. Is there a sequence and development chart?
6. Is there anything missing? Does it satisfy the requirements of the National Curriculum?
7. What is the cost of the material?

Pupils' materials

1. Is the format: attractive/compact/easy to handle/robust/colourful/stimulating/enjoyable?
2. Is the presentation: logical/clear?
3. Are the situations in the text suitable for: boys and girls/ the social background of your pupils/ the ethnic mix of your pupils?
4. Are there sufficient opportunities for practice: practical skills/written skills/ mental skills/calculator skills?
5. Is the content: comprehensive/developmental/appropriate?
6. Is there sufficient opportunity to: extend the able/support the less able?
7. Does the scheme allow for: exposition by the teacher/discussion/practical work/ practice and consolidation/investigational work/problem-solving?

Assessment material

1. Is it suitable for: diagnosis/planning a pupil's programme of work?
2. Does the scheme allow for a suitable record-keeping system?
3. Do the materials and record-keeping system meet the requirements of the national assessment procedures?

Readability

1. Is the readability level appropriate?
2. Is the print size suitable?
3. Is the layout clear and uncluttered?
4. Is the vocabulary appropriate to age and ability?
5. Are the mathematical terms clearly explained?

Teacher's manuals

1. Does it give sufficient advice about organizing and using the scheme?
2. Does it give ideas for introductory/practical/enrichment work?
3. Does it give information about resources?
4. Does it give answers to pupils' texts?

Any other comments

9
MANAGING RESOURCES FOR A MATHEMATICAL ENVIRONMENT

Introduction

Have you looked at a dictionary definition of the verb to manage? One definition says that it is the process of contriving successfully to achieve some object. So in order to be a successful manager it is necessary to know what is being managed and why.

In the context of this discussion some of the materials that must be managed are:

1. maths equipment, both commercial (such as rulers, calculators and scales) and home-made;
2. published schemes;
3. teachers' reference books;
4. mathematics resource books;
5. games and activities both teacher-made and bought;
6. stationery materials, such as squared paper, isometric paper;
7. collections of other useful materials.

Managing equipment and resources

The management of such a diverse collection of materials entails:

1. keeping abreast of recent developments;
2. consulting the staff;

3. making decisions about and ordering new materials, bearing in mind safety criteria;
4. storing materials systematically so that they can be easily retrieved;
5. checking, maintaining and repairing equipment.

Keeping abreast of recent developments

If you do not already belong to either the Association of Teachers of Mathematics or the Mathematical Association, join one of them and attend their conferences. These conferences will provide you with lots of new, exciting ideas for mathematics teaching; they also provide you with an opportunity to meet and talk to people in the same position as yourself.

Go on local courses, and always try to persuade another member of the staff to go with you. This provides you with many golden opportunities for informal discussion in the staffroom. It is this informal discussion in the staffroom that is often the most effective stimulus for change (see discussion item 1 in the appendix at the end of this chapter).

Consulting the staff

Basically there are two ways of consulting your colleagues: formally and informally; use both.

To make the most of informal 'chats' around the school, it is important here to gain the reputation of being a 'good listener'. People will then tell you their problems and triumphs and you will not only be able to give advice on the spot, but also gain an insight into your colleagues' strengths and weaknesses.

Remember, when consulting your colleagues about a particular decision, given them time to think it over and choose a sensible time to ask them for their considered opinion (in other words not 2 minutes before the end of playtime).

Never waste an opportunity. If new stock or books arrive in the school, do not hide in your room to open them. Wait until there are lots of colleagues in the staffroom and open your parcel with a fuss. Few people can resist curiosity about the contents of a parcel.

More formally, consultation with staff on minor mathematical matters can be dealt with in general staff meetings. More time-consuming issues (such as the planning of a new mathematics scheme) have to be dealt with in special staff meetings possibly using directed days. In a large school it may be necessary to organize 'committees' to concentrate on particular areas of whatever concern is currently being dealt with. As maths co-ordinator you, of course, would be expected to attend all the committees.

A questionnaire can be a very useful device for formally eliciting the opinion of your colleagues on particular issues, for example, their opinion of a mathematics scheme, or some materials. These questionnaires should be short and to the point, and not too frequent. People always think more carefully about an opinion if they are going to write it down on paper. Once they have been handed in you can go to a staff meeting/meeting with the head with some tangible proof of the opinions of your colleagues (see discussion item 2 in the appendix to this chapter).

Making decisions about and ordering new materials

This must be done in consultation with the staff. Few teachers will happily use materials imposed on them.

If there is any doubt expressed about 'new materials' order a small amount as a taster and tempt people into using it by suggesting particular successful activities with it (be ready with follow-ups).

There is little point in flooding the school with wonderful equipment if it is only to gather dust in cupboards. You can always order more if it proves popular and useful. It is also better to introduce new equipment slowly, a piece at a time, and make sure it is being used effectively than to introduce a lot all at once. Some reasons for this are:

1. It is probably the only way the school can afford it.
2. It keeps the impetus of new equipment coming in regularly over a long period of time. Teachers will get into the habit of regularly discussing something to do with mathematics. These discussions can, without threat, be broadened out into other areas of mathematics teaching.
3. Frequently when a lot of new equipment/books arrive at once something gets neglected and pushed to the back of the cupboard. Schools and children cannot afford this kind of circumstantial neglect.

Choosing new materials involves some consideration of the 'safety' of mathematics equipment, for example, selecting safe compasses, ordering plastic pinboards, using plastic see-through bottles rather than glass for capacity work, etc.

Storing materials systematically for easy retrieval

The location of equipment and resources should bear in mind

1. the geography of the school:

    (a) how many floors does the building have?

(b) how many and where are the stock cupboards?
(c) are there any outlying buildings?
(d) is there a library?
(e) are there any resource areas?

Within the restrictions of the architecture of the school and existing provisions, materials should obviously be stored so that they can be adequately catalogued. Other considerations include:

2. the organization of the teaching: is it open-plan, combined classes, traditional class teaching, group teaching? These considerations may influence your decisions about the range of materials that can be located in the classrooms, which materials can be kept on long-term loan and which on short-term loan. Combined with this criteria is the nature of the equipment;
3. the age range of the classes: especially year grouping or family grouping;
4. the autonomy of the children: are the children allowed freedom of access to the resources as part of the policy of the school, or is access always restricted to the staff? If so could this be changed? Any system that encourages children to take any responsibility for their own learning depends on its success on making the children as independent of the teacher as possible. Make sure that children know where everything is kept and establish the fact that everything has to be replaced after use.

What is the present situation? Does it need to be changed? Both the physical set-up and staff attitudes to such matters as sharing and mutual support may have to be changed. Does the present situation suggest that initially there must be a pooling of materials gathered over the years?

Are the quantities of resources available adequate and how readily are new supplies obtainable?

Try to respond in a rational way to each of the above questions. Discuss them, at length if necessary, with your colleagues as co-operation is by far the least stressful mode of working. Prepare visual aids in the form of charts or flow diagrams to illustrate the various alternative ways of doing things and display these in the staffroom so that the staff can comment upon them (see discussion item 3 in the appendix at the end of this chapter).

Storing equipment

Obviously the different resources/materials require different storage schemes.

Maths equipment

In an open-plan/semi-open-plan school with co-operative teaching, and where a high degree of child autonomy is encouraged, the most sensible system is to have a mathematics 'bay' where all the mathematical needs for the area served are catered for.

However, the majority of primary schools have buildings with separate classrooms, corridors, halls and stockrooms. Even if the school could afford to equip every classroom with all the mathematical resources that the children might use in a year, it would be impossible to store it all in the classroom.

Some of the alternatives are as follows:

1. Each classroom has a basis of 'core' equipment and the rest is kept in a stockroom, catalogued, possibly with a signing-out system incorporating some form of agreement between teachers (on a fortnightly basis) about who is going to have what in their classroom.
2. Each classroom has a basis of 'core' equipment, but also some extra items to 'look after' which the class teacher has responsibility for. Every teacher has a list of the equipment each classroom has and sends for what she requires from the appropriate classroom. The advantage of this over the last alternative is that stockrooms require constant organization, locking and unlocking, and are not usually suitable places to send children to look for things.
3. Every classroom has a basis of 'core' equipment as before, but this time the co-ordinator (yourself) looks after any additional equipment and teachers apply to you for anything extra they need. The advantage of this system is you know who is using what and when and so can offer possible extension activities.

What should constitute 'core' equipment? This depends upon what resources the school already has and how much money is available to extend these resources. So whereas we might consider a pair of good bucket balances as essential equipment for a primary classroom it may have to be a piece of shared equipment in your circumstances, even if only temporarily, while waiting for more money. Basically each member of staff has to decide, with your advice, what they consider 'core' equipment for their classroom should comprise.

The mathematical equipment in each classroom can be kept in cupboards, on shelves etc. or it can be kept on a mathematics trolley – these can be an alternative organizing device. The trolleys can be collected in yearly and restocked to suit the new age group in the classroom. They can also be a means for classes to share equipment as they can be wheeled around. As mathematics consultant you can check materials and equipment in each class very easily by asking for the trolleys to be sent to you.

If you have decided to reorganize the school equipment, it may be that you have the delicate task of persuading everybody to pool their equipment and share it out again. This can be a very difficult task because people who have 'built up' and looked after their equipment for years may not wish at all to share it with others. To be realistic, you may not be able to persuade them to part with it all, so be prepared to make compromises (for example, putting them in charge of these particular items).

Published schemes

The storage of published schemes depends upon the school's use of these schemes. If children have their own workbooks or textbooks there is little problem from the storage point of view. These can be stored in each child's personal storage space and any spares in the stockroom. However, from the mathematics education point of view, children who are merely working their way through a published mathematics scheme are having a narrow and impoverished experience of mathematics learning.

If the school's scheme of work suggests that children may at different times use several published schemes then there are various possibilities.

1. In an open-plan type school, they could be kept in the mathematics bay.
2. In a traditional type school each class could have a selection of the necessary books with a back-up collection to cater for sudden 'runs'. This back-up collection could be kept in:

    (a) a stockroom;
    (b) the library;
    (c) the staffroom;
    (d) the same place as the reading scheme; or
    (e) a special resource area for mathematics.

Alternatively, each member of staff could take responsibility for a different area of the scheme or in the final resort, you could look after all the extra books and children could fetch them from your classroom (not ideal).

Teachers' reference books

These can be kept, either by the teachers using them, or in the staffroom where they can easily be referred to at playtime, or in whatever location other teachers' reference books are kept.

Mathematics resource books

These can be kept in the staffroom, the library, a mathematics resource area, or shared around the staff as long as everybody either knows what everybody else has, or there are opportunities for frequent exchange.

Games and other home-made activities

It is easier to store games and activities if they are of similar sizes. Gestetner sell 'board' which is thin A4 card that comes in many colours. This board can be hand-fed through a Banda machine, which makes manufacture of the same game faster.

In a set of games activities, particularly games with many small pieces, it is a wise plan to make each game out of a different colour card, so that stray pieces can easily be assigned to their correct place. If games are kept in plastic bags wrongly assigned pieces can easily be identified.

There are resealable freezer bags available from good hardware shops that are just the right size for A4 card. These are see-through and ideal for storing games. These bags are best labelled using adhesive envelope labels.

Larger games can be made by taping several sheets of this card together. Up to four pieces will still fold up easily and fit into one of these bags. The bags can then be stored either in trays, or in pamphlet boxes (for the impecunious school with willing parents/assistants these can be made out of washing powder boxes covered in wallpaper). These trays or pamphlet boxes can also be labelled using adhesive envelope labels.

As some games and activities may be very specific to particular age ranges/classes they will probably be kept in the relevant classrooms. Other activities may be specific to particular chapters in books, or especially designed to be used alongside another piece of equipment – for example, sorting cards with logic-blocks.

For very large games and activity cards again try to keep to the same colours for each game and to similar sizes, for example, A1 or A2. Keep each game in a plastic bag.

Very large pieces of card will have to be kept in a map chest or a poster rail, otherwise the card will get crumpled. Such large pieces of furniture have to be kept where there is room for them, for example, stockroom, staffroom, resource area, your classroom.

There is no perfect system for storing mathematics resources: each school has to evolve its own organization according to its circumstances and needs. The organization of resources should encourage child autonomy. The children should know where things are, how to get what they need and should learn to put things back in the right place when they have finished with them. However, we do not want children to spend the whole day fetching and carrying.

It is important that the storage system in your school is evolved with the agreement of the staff, and that once it has been chosen it is monitored and if necessary completely changed.

Stationery materials

Even if stationery materials have been especially purchased for use in mathematics the best storage for this type of material is wherever stationery is normally kept in the school.

Other materials

Other materials (for example, corks, zips, conkers, etc.) are best kept scattered around classrooms with each teacher having a list of who has what, so that it can be sent for when needed.

Checking, repairing and maintaining equipment

This involves:

1. Inspecting the equipment and resources regularly (at least once a year, but not necessarily all at once).
2. Throwing out broken equipment that is irreparable, organizing the repair of equipment you cannot do yourself and ordering replacement equipment.
3. Collecting incomplete games and activities and reorganizing them to make complete sets.
4. Organizing sessions to replace worn-out games.
5. Perusing all books, workcards and booklets, throwing out and replacing those beyond redemption, and organizing the mending of the slightly damaged.
6. If the teachers have a core of books and equipment in their rooms, these will have to be reassessed yearly to cater for any changes in age range.

Managing the scheme of work

Chapter 8 dealt with choosing a published scheme of work and designing your own scheme in detail, so here we only remind you of some of the management tasks connected with implementing the scheme.

In this context the scheme of work does not mean the chosen published scheme of work although it may include a published scheme, or indeed, parts of more than one.

The mathematics scheme of work is a set of guidelines designed to help teachers in the school plan their children's mathematical activities so as to involve them in a range of experiences across the breadth of the curriculum that is appropriate to them. It is designed to promote a common ethos in the mathematical teaching and learning throughout the school.

Some of the most successful and most worthwhile schemes of work are designed by the staff themselves. Sometimes the scheme uses a commercially published set of texts or workcards as the core material, but can be designed completely independently of any published material. As we said in Chapter 7 this can be a difficult but rewarding task. One fruitful way to tackle the preparation of a scheme is small groups of teachers to take responsibility for different areas of the curriculum. The new scheme of work is then introduced to the staff as a whole. This may take the form of each group presenting a brief report which can then be generally discussed.

However, this is not always possible to arrange. If the scheme of work has been in the main written by yourself then you will have to go through it all in staff meetings, offering your colleagues every opportunity to discuss it. Even if you are designing the scheme you should introduce each area to the staff before it is finally written up so that ideas brought up in discussion can be incorporated in the final product (see Chapter 8).

Once a scheme has been introduced to the staff of a school then it is time to start implementing it. Implementing a new mathematics scheme in a primary school is such a major undertaking that it should be given priority over all other curriculum innovations for at least one year. Achieving this may test your powers of persuasion with your headteacher and other staff with special responsibilities, but it is worth a try!

Preparing the scheme for use

Does the scheme need home-made materials and games? In this case the first step is to make sure that there is sufficient card, felt-tips, plastic covering, etc. to enable the games and activities to be made. The second step is to organize workshops for the manufacture of these materials. A4 card can be hand-fed through a Banda, so make sure that any games that you require multiple copies of are drawn out on a Banda sheet. Use parents and older children to colour in games and non-teaching assistants to cover them. Remember to make decisions about storage systems before you make the games so that they fit into your storage systems. Making games and home-made equipment is very time-consuming so it is well worth considering buying ready-made anything that is available and that fits into your scheme.

Does the scheme require a lot of stationery items like squared paper and isometric paper? If so make sure that plenty is ordered.

Once the scheme has been introduced to the staff and the materials and books required for it have arrived, these need to be distributed about the school so as to allow the children ready access to them. The home-made materials have started to be made, so it is now time to introduce the children to the scheme. You will have to discuss with your colleagues how the scheme will be introduced – the whole school at once, only in the first-year classes, or only in selected classes.

The whole school at once

The advantage of this is that everybody will be involved and so discussions of the scheme will be interesting to everybody. The disadvantage is that the school may not have enough money suddenly to re-equip with the necessary equipment and books, so the carefully planned scheme could get off to a bad start because of a lack of basic materials.

Only in the first-year classes

The advantage of this system is that any extra money for equipment, or time for making home-made activities can be channelled each year to one particular year group and so the scheme should not fail for lack of resources. The main disadvantage of this is that it will take a long time to run through the school and both teachers and children may be deprived of the opportunity to use the new scheme.

Only in selected classes

This is a compromise, but a healthy one. As many classes as the school can afford to equip start the scheme each year until all the classes are involved. Careful selection of teachers to be involved in starting the scheme can also help it succeed in its early stages.

Do not forget the parents. Some schemes fail because the parents remain unconvinced or ignorant of the educational principles behind them. Hold a parents' evening on the new scheme to explain the principles behind it and why it is better than the old scheme. When holding a parents' evening/day, showing the parents a video of the children working has been found to be very successful.

Once the scheme is being used you need to monitor and evaluate (see Chapter 11).

Managing people

If you are a new member of staff you must initially demonstrate good teaching ability and general responsibility in the school.

It is very important to liaise closely with your headteacher; she/he is officially in charge of the curriculum and has delegated responsibility for mathematics to you. You must find out what kind of emphasis the headteacher is looking for in a mathematics curriculum. If you hope to make changes throughout the school, you will require the full support of the headteacher and you may need to be seen to have it.

You should also liaise with other subject co-ordinators. Take notice of and discuss with them (if possible) the strategies they have used in managing people in their responsibilities. If you are a new member of staff ask their advice; they will know the school a lot better than you. If this is simply a new role for you in the school ask their advice about your new role. If they are co-ordinators this probably means that they are also experienced teachers. It is important to gain the support of the senior members of staff and asking advice is always a very good way of breaking down barriers.

Be particular, not only to follow but to be seen to follow the other co-ordinators' guidelines and schemes of work. You can hardly hope for anybody to follow yours if you apparently scorn theirs. Ask other post-holders for advice in their particular areas of the curriculum.

Listen to what others have to say. Ask colleagues what their opinions are about the present situation, what they consider is successful and what changes they think are required. It is often difficult to listen to people particularly if you find it hard to agree on any point they say. However, it is very important to know and understand the views of your colleagues; a well-prepared general always studies the opposition. How can you hope to make a successful job of changing opinions and styles of teaching if you do not know what they really are in the first place, or the reasons behind them?

Listening may be difficult when you are bubbling over with new ideas that you are anxious that everyone should try out at the earliest opportunity. However, you cannot steamroller everybody into believing what *you* believe. Different people will have to be approached in different ways and it is only by talking with them, and listening to them, that you will discover the appropriate way for each colleague. The importance of listening cannot be overestimated, it enables you to make a fair assessment of the situation and also shows that you value other people's opinions.

Always be prepared to give people time. In particular spend time with probationary teachers and teachers coming back into the service after a period away. If you are prepared to give freely of your time people will bring their problems and their successes to you.

If people ask for help with a particular problem, be assiduous in giving it, even if you feel it is an unimportant issue. It is either important to the teacher concerned or they have something else they wish to talk to you about and this is an easy way in for them. You will also be building the foundations for discussing more important issues.

Should you feel that your colleagues are in general complacent about a less than wonderful situation, then you may need to create a desire for change. This can be done in several ways. For instance, by:

1. giving a short talk on the APU findings;
2. leading a discussion on the Cockcroft Report;
3. organizing a study of the HMI discussion document *National Curriculum documents and non-statutory guidance*, and a comparison of its recommendations with what is happening mathematically in your school;
4. inviting your local mathematics advisory teacher to give a talk on the authority's mathematics guidelines;
5. planning a parents' day/evening on problem-solving or practical mathematics. It is amazing how motivating the thought of parents coming in can be. Teachers immediately find the need to discuss mathematical ideas with you and their colleagues so that they are clear in their own minds about exactly what they will say to parents;
6. getting hold of a video showing children happy and active doing mathematics and discuss it with your staff. Videos give staff the opportunity of discussing a shared experience.

Enlist the children's support. If you have a class of children enjoying and participating in good mathematics, send them out around the school like disciples to show other classes interesting and exciting things they have been doing. Lend them out to other teachers to lead problem-solving sessions. Display and encourage other members of staff to display interesting and exciting mathematics around the school.

Remember many teachers find mathematics a very sensitive area of the curriculum. It is frequently the subject that they are least happy with. Change can be very threatening, particularly when it challenges the habits of a lifetime. So try to lead by example; initiate small changes at first, not big ones. 'Bottom-up' curriculum innovation is frequently the most successful (see in-service training, p. 128).

If the school uses a published scheme that you do not approve of, do not attempt to throw away all the books in the first week. This move would be very likely to prove unpopular. Many teachers find it hard to teach mathematics without following a published mathematics scheme. At first tempt teachers into doing additional activities which could help compensate for the disadvantages of the scheme; offer them proven ideas and additional texts. Make them dissatisfied with the scheme themselves by discussing aims and objectives of mathematics teaching (using the Cockcroft Report, HMI document *Mathematics 5-16* or the National Curriculum documents as a basis). Look at the scheme to see if it fulfils the aims and objectives. If possible try to put them in the position of asking you to send for inspection copies of other schemes.

Start by looking at the resources of the school. It is useful to know what resources are available and it is also non-threatening. It is the easiest way into somebody's classroom, a foot in the door. Ask teachers what resources they think they are lacking. Order new resources and negotiate 10 minutes of normal staff meeting time to discuss how they can be used. This may be the first time you have had to lead staff discussions and it is a good idea to let yourself in gently. Discussing resources can lead on to more important matters.

Invite your local mathematics advisory teacher to come and give a talk on some mathematical issues. Demonstrate that outsiders are interested in how the school is functioning mathematically and that you have strong outside support, that you are not alone in trying to initiate changes and that these changes are being recommended across the authority and indeed across the country. A school that took no notice of these changes would be failing its pupils.

If your teachers feel unsure and unhappy about problem-solving and investigations, lead some sessions in which you give them the opportunity to have a go themselves. Ask them to try out the same examples on their children and report back to a staff meeting. It may mean that you could end up with the whole school doing polyominoes but that does not matter.

If your teachers are worried about the organization of mathematical activities, organize visits to your classroom while the children are involved in mathematical activities (after you have set up your ideal mathematical environment). Do not worry about it running absolutely perfectly. If things go wrong, talk about it with the teacher; you can both learn from your mistakes and, in any case, perfection can be rather daunting. You will gain more converts if you admit that you still have a long way to go yourself. Invite constructive criticism of yourself. If you invite it, it may be more constructive than if your visitor goes away to gossip with other colleagues.

Do not expect teachers to change everything all at once. Worthwhile change is necessarily a slow, well-thought-out process. Nobody should be expected to change both the style and content of their teaching at the same time and demanding it will create insecurity. Remember to give praise to teachers when it is due as adults need praise just as much as children.

To sum up, good person-management involves above all listening, then tactful action based upon all the information that you have elicited. It involves you asking advice as well as giving it. It involves making sure that everyone is well aware that you have the full force of the head/advisory teachers/inspectorate behind you. Last, and certainly not least, it involves time and effort on your part. Time to give the teachers and effort in making sure that they are aware that you are prepared to give them the time whenever they need it.

School-based in-service training (INSET)

School-based in-service training (INSET) can be broadly divided into three types, informal, semi-formal and formal. You should try to make full use of all three types.

Informal

This tends to be 'bottom-up', dealing with problems as they arise. It is friendly, can be lively and is frequently the most effective. It includes looking at new books and equipment as they arrive in the staffroom, or indeed looking at forgotten pieces of equipment as you dig them out from the back of the stockroom. It also involves always making the most of informal staffroom discussion, and many of the ideals discussed in managing people. Opportunities for school-based in-service training also arise when mounting mathematics displays around the school, when organizing mathematics competitions and through featuring mathematics in assembly. All these activities are designed to stimulate interest and enthusiasm in maths in both children and teachers and create a stimulating mathematical environment.

The mounting of mathematics displays around the school

There is a wide variety of mathematical displays that can be mounted and they are well worth the time and energy involved. First, and probably the most important, are displays of the children's work. These attract particular attention if they are augmented by photographs of the children doing the work. Encourage other teachers to add to the display. Some schools have topic-based displays around the school. Make sure that mathematics gets its fair share of display space or time.

If you ask children 'why do you learn mathematics?', or 'what is mathematics for?', they typically reply 'to pass exams or pass tests'. If they see any links with adult life it is likely to be money. It is very important that children are convinced that mathematics has a place in the real world. Invite people in, go out and photograph people at work, collect posters of people using mathematics in the real world and put up displays of the results.

Invite parents and other interested adults to add to the displays. Through their trades and professions they will be able to demonstrate various uses of mathematics at work, for instance:

1. scaffolding erectors and their use of 3, 4, 5-triangles, particularly good if you have some putting up scaffolding around the school;
2. joiners;
3. chemists (ask them to bring their pill-counting tray – triangular numbers);
4. architects;
5. seamstresses, designers, and tailors;
6. mechanics;
7. cooks, etc.

Mathematics topics particularly suitable for displays

Number: Children find large numbers fascinating and will show great interest in a display of large numbers of things, for example, jars of dried beans, bags of conkers, a cheese of matchsticks, a display of a million dots (available from Tarquin), photos of large numbers of people, a 1,000-number line (this can be left up in the hall as the children find it very useful). A charitable activity linked to this is the setting up of a penny line round the school.

Shape: Geometry provides obvious opportunities for a variety of displays, from photos of shapes in the environment (photolinks), to displays of junk models.

Pattern: Number patterns, tessellations, wallpaper design, etc.

Measurement: Collections of measuring instruments old and new (this might be linked with adults who work with the instruments coming in to demonstrate them). A historical display of 'old-fashioned' units (feet and inches, cubits, etc.).

Mathematics fairs

Many LEAs organize an annual mathematics fair for their schools. Try to persuade your colleagues that your school should contribute. Arranging a visit to the fair can provide the incentive to get people interested for the following year. Besides being a focus for in-service work, contributing to a mathematics fair may provoke the more inflexible of your colleagues to reconsider their teaching approaches.

Mathematics competitions

Some children can become very excited by weekly mathematics competitions. The problem is not getting children interested but thinking up enough new ideas. The children can be very disappointed when there is no competition. The nature of the prize is usually of little importance, but it is a good idea to read out the solution and prizewinner in assembly.

Once the idea of mathematics competitions is firmly established in the school, enlist the help of the children and their parents in helping to look for, think up and set up competitions.

Try to involve *all* the school staff in the competitions including the dinner ladies and the school caretaker. You should use these competitions to create an atmosphere of interest in mathematics and that means everybody being interested in mathematics.

Ideas for competitions

Estimate, for example, how many buttons in a jar? How many matchsticks in a cheese? How much water will fit into a barrel? How long is a ball of wool? etc. These competitions are always popular and it is not necessarily the older children who come closest to the answer. Obviously the buttons have to be counted, or the barrel measured, and these tasks can be given to different classes in turn to do.

Think up collection competitions, for example, how many different small things can be fitted into a matchbox? Who can collect the largest number of conkers? (The conkers can be collected afterwards and used as mathematics equipment for counting and weighing.)

Competitions can be taken from mathematical posters; examples usually involve counting, looking for differences, odd ones out, etc.

Mathematics in assembly

Mathematics can be included in assembly in many guises. It certainly includes the showing of good mathematical work, but can also involve the demonstration of mathematical abilities, for instance with young children counting or, with older children, any child who has remarkable number-bond recall could demonstrate it.

Solutions to problems that can be demonstrated by children moving can be performed in assembly, for example, Frogs and the Fifteen puzzle. The 'Fifteen' puzzle with 35 children is particularly impressive.

Assembly is the obvious place to introduce a new competition and read the results from the old one. It is also the obvious place to have adults from the outside world talk about how they use mathematics. Do not forget to invite your school's cook, secretary and caretaker to contribute.

Children frequently perform small plays in assembly. Try to get them to perform mathematical plays, including funny ones based on common mathematical misunderstandings, for instance writing numbers incorrectly. Younger children can act out mathematical rhymes, for example, five currant buns.

Assemblies by their very nature tend to be full of regularly repeated activities. This is not necessarily a bad thing. However, get mathematics in on the act if possible. For example have children count up the pupils in their class every day and add them all up so that every day it is known how many children are in assembly. At the end of each day's assembly read the time.

Semi-formal

This involves all the organized work done by teachers that is not specifically labelled in-service training, for example, all the work related to designing a new mathematics scheme, the work related to choosing a new published scheme (see Chapter 8), preparing for a parents' evening on mathematics, co-operative teaching in mathematics and visiting other classes and schools.

Preparing for a parents' evening on mathematics

Problems are often caused for children in mathematics learning because the expectations of their parents in this area of the curriculum are not necessarily the same as the expectations of the school.

Ways of teaching mathematics and indeed the mathematics taught alters as technology advances and more research is done into children's learning. Parents frequently expect that their children will be taught and will need the same skills and knowledge that they were taught at school. It is an unsatisfactory arrangement for there to be conflicts of interest in such an important area of the children's schooling. Therefore, it is important to talk to the parents and explain what you are teaching the children, and why, and how they can help their children. Parents' evenings can be a way of communicating to a large number of parents at once. Parents also appreciate a booklet on mathematics teaching in the school with ideas on how they can help their children.

Parents' evenings need a lot of preparation, and they must be seen to involve all the staff so that the parents know that all the teachers in the school are working towards common goals.

Co-operative teaching in mathematics

Due to high pupil–teacher ratios this is not always possible, but if it is, then co-operative teaching can be very fruitful. Teachers all too rarely have the opportunity of discussing their teaching with another involved and interested party. Two teachers also provide more than twice the number of ideas between them by airing and discussing issues.

Another teacher may be able to explain something to a child where the first teacher has failed. Providing the child with a different slant on the problem may be all that is necessary to help him/her over the obstacle.

Co-operative teaching can allow the class teacher the opportunity to work uninterrupted with a single child or group who need particular help.

Visiting other classes and schools

Visiting other classes in the school enables staff to share ideas and to become a more cohesive team in their mathematics teaching.

Visiting other schools should not be arranged in a haphazard fashion or little may be gained from it. Visits should be arranged with particular objectives in mind. Likely objectives are:

1. to see a scheme of work the school is considering buying in use;
2. to view different methods of organization of classes of mathematics learning or different methods of organization of maths resources;
3. to look at how a school sets up good mathematical displays;
4. to see a system of recording in practice.

This does not mean discouraging the teachers from looking at anything else, but it does give them something particular to look at, discuss and report back on.

It is very important that teachers who have visited other schools are given the opportunity to report back on what they saw.

Formal

Formal in-service training within the school tends to be 'top down' and usually takes place in compulsory staff meetings at lunchtime, after school or occasionally during school time (possibly during hymn practice or on directed days). The advantage of lunchtime and hymn practice meetings is that everybody can attend easily. The disadvantage is that the time available is usually rather too short to allow major issues to be dealt with. The disadvantage of after-school meetings is that some teachers may find it difficult to attend and they can go on too long. The advantage is that they can be longer. In some schools the head is willing to take a singing practice with the whole school at the end of the day so that the teachers can actually start their meeting in school time. Obviously directed days provide the best opportunity for formal in-service education with your colleagues, but you will not be able to book them all for mathematics!

You can organize this type of in-service training in a variety of different ways. You can give talks or you can run workshops. Activities might include:

1. discussions on topics like teaching styles or the aims and objectives of maths teaching;
2. trying out new equipment, for example, explanation and discussion of practical activities with multibases;
3. doing some mathematics;
4. looking at and discussing videos of children doing mathematics (giving teachers a shared experience);
5. making games and activities, and discussing their use.

You can invite outside speakers in to speak to the staff – say equipment specialists or the advisory teacher.

If you arrange such a staff meeting remember that you are taking up people's precious time, so make sure you are very well prepared so that the staff feel that your meetings are worth attending.

Assessment and testing

Assessment and testing are fundamental to the implementation of the National Curriculum (see Chapter 10). This testing is a combination of national tests (standard assessment tasks – SATS) and teacher assessment (TA). Schools must decide the form of the tasks to be set for teacher assessment. These can be chosen from published materials, from local sources or designed by you and your colleagues.

To reach a consensus on what tests are to be used will involve you in gathering information from a variety of sources and in considerable discussion with your colleagues. This activity can provide the opportunity for in-service training as not only will there be an exchange of ideas about carrying out the assessments, but it will lead naturally to discussion about aims and objectives and about teaching approaches.

The necessity to moderate the results of standard assessment tasks and teacher assessment in a meeting with other teachers from your local area will require you and your colleagues to analyse critically your own procedures – again a form of in-service training.

Other in-service activities

It is also important that you encourage colleagues to attend in-service courses out of school. If possible encourage them to attend in pairs so that they can discuss and develop their ideas together after the course has finished. Always try to provide the opportunity for them to share their experiences and ideas with the rest of the staff (see discussion item 1 in the appendix to this chapter).

Summary

In this chapter we have looked at some of the managerial responsibilities that you may have to undertake. In particular you are likely to have responsibility for:

1. managing the mathematics equipment, its acquisition and storage;
2. the scheme of work (whether based on published texts or entirely school-designed);
3. in-service training in mathematics.

To carry out this managerial role successfully requires that you are, of course, well-organized but also, more importantly, that you are able to communicate with your colleagues and receptive to both their concerns and their advice.

Another major area of managerial responsibility – assessment and record-keeping – is considered in the next chapter.

APPENDIX: DISCUSSION ITEMS 1, 2 AND 3

Discussion item 1

A mathematics centre in London had a policy of asking two members of staff from each school to attend courses. This was because they discovered that when one member of staff went on a course they rarely reported back to the rest of the staff. However, when two members of staff went on a course they nearly always talked about it in the staffroom, initially between themselves then involving others.

It is also easier to keep up attendance on a course when there is more than one of you.

Discussion item 2

Should we buy **** equipment?

1. Have you looked at it? (It is available for perusal in the staffroom.)
2. Do you think it can be used in ways which agree with our aims and objectives for mathematics teaching?
3. If yes, can you give some concise examples, possibly quoting aims?
4. Does it fit in with our mathematics scheme?
5. If yes, give examples.
6. Do you think it is an essential piece of equipment for your classroom?
7. Do you think it will significantly improve the children's learning experience in mathematics?
8. Should we buy it?
9. How many?

Discussion item 3

Advantages and disadvantages of possible sitings for alternative resources

	Advantages	Disadvantages
Staffroom (possibly with a signing-out book)	Available to all teachers	Nobody even notices them, they become 'wallpaper' Once they have left the staffroom they never come back
Library	Available to all teachers and children The library ticket system makes sure they are returned from time to time	Teachers forget about them Many of them are not initially interesting to children so they may be ignored

In classrooms around the school (list in staffroom)	They will get used by the teacher who has them	List gets lost under union notices so teachers do not know who has got what and, if you do not see something regularly you only occasionally remember its existence
In stockrooms or resource area	The resources are available to all	Communal areas and stockrooms are very difficult to keep tidy and organized People forget to bring things back

10
ASSESSMENT AND RECORD-KEEPING

Introduction

Effective assessment could be said to be at the heart of good teaching and learning. Used well it can provide a reliable feedback to help guide us in our work as teachers and offer useful information to the various groups concerned with the children and the school. Assessment can take many forms and can serve different purposes. The styles of assessment presently employed in primary schools often include:

1. the use of discussion, questioning, listening and observation;
2. setting up particular tasks with built-in checking-up procedures, such as the ILEA checkpoints scheme;
3. regular marking of recorded work;
4. informal on-the-spot testing;
5. formal or standardized tests.

When choosing the most appropriate assessment instrument one needs to consider carefully the purpose of the proposed assessment. For example, it may be that the assessment is to give children information about how they are doing. Perhaps it is needed by teachers to enable them to see how the children in their class are progressing; or to provide information to parents, the governing body of the school, the local education authority or the government.

What should you test?

One of the crucial issues here is the question of validity of the test, that is to say, its appropriateness to the situation for which it is being used. The content and style of the assessment procedure must relate well to what you want to find out. For example, we often use assessment in primary mathematics and the results tell us what children do not know – but is that what we set out to find out? If we compare that with the new approaches being adopted for older pupils, for instance in GCSE, the emphasis is placed on finding out what the candidates can do through the use of well-defined criteria for assessment.

There are obvious dangers in overuse and misuse of assessment. Mathematics is one subject that generally tends to be overassessed, perhaps sometimes because it is often very easy to use mathematics tests as a means of providing breathing space for the teacher. But it must be recognized that assessment for its own sake is very questionable! Overassessing pupils can have really damaging effects. The most important ones are that it can discourage pupils and that it may colour the view of mathematics held by pupils, by parents and by teachers.

In practice the ground rules have now been established for us. The National Curriculum and its attendant testing procedures will determine the modes and styles and timing of national assessment. However, some element of teacher assessment will still be an important requirement and will have to be determined by the teachers concerned.

It is likely to become the responsibility of the mathematics co-ordinator or post-holder in conference with the headteacher to be conversant with and organize for the National Curriculum assessment procedures and schedule. This task will involve communicating to and with others including colleagues, parents and governors, – taking responsibility for the administration, possible moderation and reporting procedures as well as perhaps an evaluation of the results with regard to your particular school.

Since the removal of the 11+ in the early 1970s many schools or local education authorities have filled the gap by introducing some form of formal testing. There is a variety of standardized commercial tests available for this purpose which are in regular use, for example, Richmond, Yardsticks, NFER and of course some LEAs have developed their own. The ages at which children are tested varies from LEA to LEA but generally speaking it is not before the ages of 8+.

So, assessment through the form of standardized tests is not a new phenomenon. It is widely believed that as many as 50 per cent of LEAs use this form of testing at some stage of primary schooling. However, the purposes to which the results are put varies greatly. The big difference between what happens now and the National Curriculum assessment procedures is the compulsory nature of testing at the reporting stages of 7, 11, 14 and 16 for all but statemented pupils. Thus this kind of testing takes on a much more formal mantle.

The National Curriculum model for mathematics looks like this (Fig 10.1):

Figure 10.1

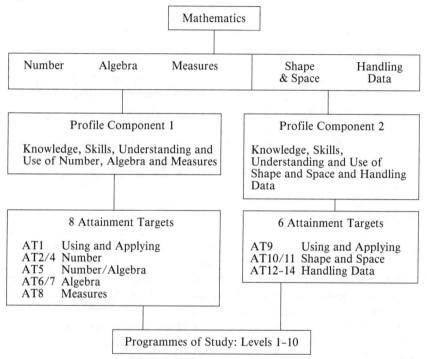

What assessment procedures are required?

As the diagram shows the range of attainment targets is grouped into two profile components drawing on the five areas of mathematics shown: number, algebra, measures, space and shape, and handling data. These targets help you as a teacher to attribute a level to represent a 'stage of learning' for each child for each of the three profile components for mathematics. There are ten possible levels to cater for children in the age-range 5–16.

In determining the levels for each child you are required to attribute a teacher assessment element and each child also obtains a result from the standard assessment tasks (SATS) that they have been required to carry out in class. These tasks are sent to the school by an outside body, and involve a range of tasks: some extended, some long and some short. These definitions will be clarified by the National Curriculum Council in due course. For primary-age children this assessment only applies to children aged 7 and 11 years.

The results of the teacher assessment and the standard assessment tasks will need to be aggregated in some way – this is yet to be determined. It will also be necessary for members from schools or groups of schools to meet at some stage to engage in a moderation process. This is necessary to ensure that the standards are the same across teachers and schools. This sort of moderation procedure has been in use for the secondary examinations, GCE, CSE and now GCSE, for some time.

Before you can assist your colleagues in making sense of all this and in interpreting and implementing the assessment procedures in your school you will need to clarify for yourself how all the pieces fit together. A glossary of terms and simple explanations of each is provided to help you with this task (Table 10.1).

Table 10.1

Attainment Targets (ATs) – the set of objectives for each foundation subject (including core subjects), which sets out the knowledge, skills and understanding that pupils of different abilities and maturities are expected to develop within that subject. There are 10 levels of attainment defined by means of appropriate statements.

Level of Attainment – The 10 different levels of achievement reflecting differences in ability and in progress defined within each target.

Statements of Attainment – specific objectives given for each of the 10 levels of attainment within any target or set of targets. They cover all four Key stages from 5–16 years.

Programme of Study (PoS) – What children need to be taught in order to reach the objectives as set out in the attainment targets defined for each Key stage.

Key Stage – A period within compulsory schooling towards the end of which children's performance is assessed and reported. There are four: 5–7, 7–11, 11–14 and 14–16.

Reporting Age – Age at which children are to be assessed and reported upon namely 7, 11, 14 and 16.

Assessment arrangements – The arrangements for assessment which will show what pupils have achieved in relation to the attainment targets at each Key stage. A variety of assessment methods including some form of 'task' testing (SAT) and continuous assessment by teachers may be used.

Standard Assessment Task (SAT) – Tasks prescribed externally which may incorporate a range of assessment methods.

Profile Component (PC) – For mathematics the 14 attainment targets are grouped into two PCs. Profile Component 1 includes targets 1–8 and Profile Component 2 includes targets 9–16.

National Curriculum: From Policy to Practice (DES, 1989) gives further information, including a timetable detailing when the various assessments will be implemented.

You will need to think carefully about and prepare for an in-service training programme to induct other members of staff into the assessment procedures. A suggested model is given below.

Before you start we suggest that you make full-size overhead transparencies to represent the information given in each of the boxes. Make copies for each member of staff of the list of attainment targets given in the mathematics document. As you use each transparency talk through the various elements as fully as possible and allow time for discussion so as to clear up misunderstandings and misconceptions. If you are not sure, say so and refer back to the documents.

1. A model of our present assessment procedures:

Use this to show what you are already doing. Try to allay fears – assessment in itself is not new – for example, record cards, checking up on procedures, any school-based or LEA test etc. Discuss what the information is used for.

2.   The new national assessment procedures:

Teacher assessment (TA)	Reporting ages 7, 11, 14, 16
Standard assessment tasks (SATS)	
Explain both these elements.	

3.   What is to be tested?

Attainment targets (ATs) 14 in total – ten levels for ages 5–16 years.	What are they?
	How are they organized?
14 targets drawn from the five areas of maths:	How do they relate to the testing?
number, algebra, measures, space and shape, handling data	

Profile components used for testing procedures

PC1

including attainment targets
Using and applying number, algebra
and measures (1 AT)
Number (3 ATs)
Algebra/number (1 ATs)
Algebra (2 ATs)
Measures (1 ATs)

PC2

including attainment targets
using and applying and handling data
(1 AT)
space and shape (2 ATs)
handling data (2 ATs)

Distribute the copies of the list of attainment targets and look closely at those designed for the primary years.

Testing at 7 years

Figure 10.2

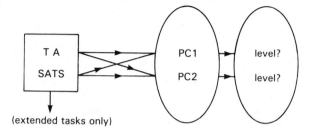

(extended tasks only)

Each child must be given a 'reported level' for each of the three profile components. At age 7 years, only levels 1, 2, 3 can be used (average 7-year-old – level 2). So for example Jane, 7, is given the profile (2, 3) at the end of the school year.

Testing at 11 years

Figure 10.3

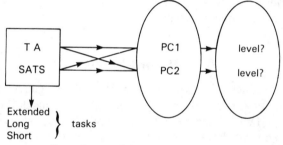

Levels 2–6 are generally to be used (average 11-year-old – level 4).

Wider dissemination of the children's attainment levels

The levels obtained by both 7-year-olds and 11-year-olds are to be communicated to their parents. Parents will also receive information in percentage form of the proportion of children achieving each level within the particular school and also the national overall results.

Teacher assessment

This element may take a variety of forms, but should be flexible and reflect your current teaching approach. It should be an ongoing process and you need to ensure that a record is kept of each pupil's progress. Some assessment of pupil's performance, measured against each of the attainment targets, will be required each term. In order to avoid the situation where there is a mismatch between the teacher assessments and standard assessment task results, you will need to keep comprehensive records on each pupil's progress in the terms when they are not required to do national testing.

It is advisable that some of your assessments are based on tasks that are similar in design to standard assessment tasks. Clearly this is desirable from the pupil's point of view – it would be very unfair suddenly to confront a pupil with a type of test or situation never before experienced. Equally important, however, is the need for you to have evidence of a pupil's performance in tests similar to standard assessment tasks if you are to arrive at a fair assessment when comparing teacher assessment and standard assessment task results.

As mathematics co-ordinator you will need to reach a consensus with your colleagues on the following:

1. the type of testing;
2. the frequency of testing;
3. the choice of test materials;
4. the format of record-keeping.

Record-keeping

With the introduction of assessment for the National Curriculum and as our schools become more and more accountable to outside bodies (parents, governors, HMIs) systematic record-keeping becomes even more of a priority. You will have to review your school's system of mathematical records. Before making any decisions about the system you and your colleagues will have to decide for whom you are recording. Your system will obviously have to work flexibly alongside those devised to meet National Curriculum assessment requirements, but here we raise general issues about keeping records.

Why record?

There is an enormous variety of reasons for recording, but two main reasons are:

1. You record so that you as a teacher can remember what the child has done, has had difficulty doing and cannot do. You need this memory aid to help you to plan each child's future work and to make sure that

all are being offered a relevant breadth and depth of mathematical experience.

2. You record so that some other teacher can read what the child has done . . . etc. so that they can make decisions about the child's future work. These 'other teachers' include the child's next teacher, any other teacher who works with the child, the head and yourself, in your role as mathematics co-ordinator. Any system of recording should be analysed according to how well it will communicate to each of these audiences.

It is important that the staff of the school agree with the reasons for recording. Remember that in some authorities parents have right of access to all their children's records.

What to record?

The possibilities are as follows.

The results of tests

If you give your children tests of any kind, printed tests or teacher-written, it would seem sensible to record the results.

Everything a child does

It can be very time-consuming to record everything a child does. Some schools have ticklists incorporated into their mathematics scheme (either commercial or school-designed) and as a child completes each task or area of work this is ticked off (see discussion items 4 and 5 in the appendix to this chapter). Some schools regulate what the children have done by 'where they are' in the mathematics scheme. In some schools children work in groups (sometimes the whole class) and it is the group's work that is recorded (ideally with any absenteeism noted).

In a school that is trying to promote child autonomy and children being involved in their own learning it is worth considering recording systems which involve the children recording what they have done, and how they did it.

Everything the child understands

From the point of view of the next teacher this is obviously an ideal type of recording but it is also the hardest because it could involve checking each child for every mathematical concept. In practice, the teacher only tests where there is doubt. Most of the time a few careful questions while the child is engaged in the activity in question will be sufficient for a teacher to discover what the child understands. The ILEA *Checkpoints* have been designed for this kind of checking and recording (see discussion item 6 in the appendix to this chapter). Other LEAs have produced similar schemes.

Anything the child cannot do

This type of record obviously has to be noted so that you can plan to give children more experiences to help them learn whatever it is they are having difficulty with.

Milestones and hiccups

This type of recording would be done alongside other types and would serve to extend the child's profile: the topics that a child was particularly good at, or had particular difficulties with.

There are always two types of recording in evidence in a school – the official recording and personal recording. Frequently they are completely separate. Ideally the personal recording should feed naturally into the official recording.

How should you record?

Types of recording vary from completely unstructured comments based upon teacher observations, to the filling in of rigid checklists ticking off tasks that the children have completed.

Unstructured observation

The advantage of this kind of assessment is that experienced teachers who know what they are looking for and who write well can communicate the child's progress and abilities very effectively.

The disadvantage of this type of report is that it gives little support to the inexperienced or apprehensive teacher and through its idiosyncratic nature can fail to communicate the child's progress and abilities.

Structured observation

Checklists   There are two types of checklist. One is a record of the mathematics a child has done. The advantage of this type of record is that it is quick, and if the original list was well thought out and balanced it can be seen at a glance what 'menu' of mathematics the children are experiencing. The disadvantage is that it does not give any clues as to how the children did the work, whether they were successful or what difficulties they had, so it may not necessarily be a help in future planning.

The other type is a checklist of what the children understand. The advantage, if the list is well-designed, is that it can give a very clear picture of what the child can do. The disadvantage of this type of record is that, unless the list *is* very well-planned, it can put teachers in the mortifying position of having children who on paper can do nothing. This can be very demoralizing for the teacher, and even more so for any parent who sees the records. Also this method offers no record of what the child *has* been doing, thus giving little support for planning.

Boxes   These are much the same as checklists (and can be used instead of either type of checklist) except space is available for comments. This method is an improvement upon simple checklists since what the children have done can be put into context, to give a more complete picture of the child and to aid planning. However, the disadvantages are that it is much more time-consuming and uses a great deal of paper.

So having decided why recording should be done, what it is you want to record, and how you would prefer to record it, you now need to look at the recording happening in your school.

Recording in the school

Is there a reasonably successful method of recording in the school? Does it accommodate to your chosen audiences? Does it actually record what you *want* to record? Does it help with planning? If it does not satisfy all of these questions, can it be adapted so that it does?

It may be that general recording in the school is excellent and only the mathematical recording is failing, in which case it may be possible to incorporate the mathematical recording into the general recording, or organize the mathematical recording on the same lines as, for instance, the reading records.

If there is no successful system of official recording in the school then one will have to be designed or chosen. This is worth taking some time over. It is unproductive to impose a method of recording, however good, because it will not succeed if the staff do not agree with it. Few endeavours fail in a school as thoroughly as an undesired recording system.

Time available for recording

When choosing or designing recording systems consideration must be given to the amount of time available for recording. Usually this is minimal. Any time in the school day used for recording is usually taken at the expense of teaching and any time outside the school day can be at the expense of preparation. It is senseless to design a wonderful recording system if it takes up too much time. Therefore, do not be too ambitious.

Choosing/designing a recording system

Start the search for a recording system with a well-planned staff meeting with handouts and visiting speakers. This will emphasize the priority that you give to this, and demonstrate your own professionalism (useful for a new member of staff or one taking on a new role).

Start the meeting by discussing why and what you (as a staff) wish to record. It is a good idea to produce a handout to give structure to the discussion (see discussion item 7 in the appendix to this chapter). Distribute it before the meeting but run through it briefly at the meeting before discussing it, and coming to a decision.

Next, you will need to look at some examples of recording systems.

Other recording systems in your school   This includes formal recording systems, for example, the school's system of reading records, and informal recording systems. Prior to the meeting ask your colleagues how they organize their personal recording. Perhaps somebody uses an excellent system that could be adapted for the whole school. Ask individual colleagues if they could describe and bring examples of their own systems.

Recording systems from other schools   Invite representatives from some of these schools to describe how their system works and the advantages and disadvantages of their system.

The local authority's recommended system   Invite a mathematics advisory teacher from your authority to advise on this system. Sufficient copies of these examples should be available for all at the meeting to peruse them. Lead the discussion on each example to decide whether it satisfies your chosen audience and if it records what you want to record.

From this point on you will have to make decisions on your feet!

Making decisions

Some of your colleagues may like particular systems, in which case it might be a good idea to suggest a trial run of the preferred systems. Alternatively your colleagues may like parts of one and parts of another, and you may have to list their preferences and go away and design a system specifically for your school.

All the same, it is extremely important that the staff of the school feel that they have collaborated in the decisions and the design of any recording system that you eventually introduce. So, you should conclude the meeting decisively; either a system has been chosen, or several examples are going to be given a trial in the school, or you have a list of ideas and with the backing of your colleagues are to go away and design a system for the school.

The next stage in your search for a recording system depends on the decisions made in the staff meeting.

1. It could involve you arranging the duplication of materials required for the trials. Get this done quickly while people are still keen to try the ideas out. If you leave it too long they will forget that they ever said they would do it.

2. Or it could involve you designing a new system based upon the decisions of the meeting. Once designed persuade some of your colleagues to give it a trial.

3. It should certainly involve you contacting the schools that your children go on to. Discuss what they require in the way of mathematical records and to what extent their demands may be met by your school. Take the minutes from your meeting and the examples that you gave your colleagues. If the teachers in your school are to put their time into building up comprehensive mathematical profiles of their pupils then they need to feel that these profiles are going to be read by the children's next teachers and that includes teachers in the next school.

The third stage is another staff meeting with all involved in the trial runs reporting back on their results. You should obviously have spoken to everybody beforehand so that you know what they are going to say.

The staff must now decide upon a system. If they are unable to decide unanimously you must go along with the majority. In the final analysis it is your decision and you must be prepared to make it.

Once the decision has been made you must arrange for the materials required to be made available, distribute them and make sure that everybody knows exactly what they are doing. It is your task to introduce the system to new members of staff and supply teachers.

Evaluating the recording system

After an agreed period of time, you should evaluate the system. This may be best accomplished by a questionnaire. If the majority are reasonably happy with the system and it seems to be working effectively then it is important to work very closely with any colleague who is dissatisfied or seems unable to work with it.

If the majority are dissatisfied and find the system difficult to implement then you must have meetings to decide if the system can be adapted or whether it is best to jettison it and return to square one.

If the system was initially successful this, unfortunately, does not mean that it will succeed for ever. So, after a period of years, it will be necessary to evaluate it again, particularly if there have been any major changes in the teaching staff.

Summary

The introduction of assessment for the National Curriculum has focused considerable attention on the testing of primary school pupils at ages 7 and 11. It would be unfortunate if, with this new emphasis, teachers forgot the real purpose of assessment and were diverted away from the good and sensible practices that most have employed for many years.

Assessing a pupil's performance should be to the benefit of both pupil and teacher. It should benefit the pupil by enabling the teacher to diagnose weaknesses in the pupil's understanding. If the pupil is to be helped to overcome any difficulties and to make progress, then this diagnosis is crucial to the teacher. Assessment should also help the teacher to evaluate the effectiveness of the learning experiences and the curriculum process. Indeed, assessment procedures should be part of the curriculum process and they should reflect the aims, objectives, criteria for content and, above all, the teaching approaches.

Much teacher assessment in the past has been incidental, but no less important for that, as it has come from close observation of children and discussion with them – both laudable, and very essential, activities. However the new arrangements will require teachers to be more systematic in their assessments and move away from informal assessment to more formal methods.

To use the system of national testing profitably, teachers will need to focus on the diagnostic by-product of their testing and to use this to help pupils develop their mathematical understanding.

Record-keeping has always been an essential part of this process. In order to provide an accurate profile of the pupils' attainments it will be even more necessary to keep records up to date and in a form that can easily be understood by other teachers. The danger is that the production of data for records may become more important than the use that is made of this information. It is up to you, as the mathematics co-ordinator, to ensure that the central importance of assessment as a means of diagnosing difficulties and of helping pupils forward is not forgotten.

References

DES (1989) *National Curriculum: From Policy to Practice*, DES, Stanmore.

ILEA (1980) *Checkpoints*, ILEA, London.

Turnbull, J. (1981, 1987) *Maths Links*, NARE Publications, Stafford.

APPENDIX: DISCUSSION ITEMS 4, 5, 6 AND 7

Discussion item 4

In one school I worked in every child had a reading record book that was a hard-backed exercise book. This book was given to them when they entered the school and stayed with them throughout their time at school. Every reading book they read was recorded in this book as well as words and sounds they had difficulty with. Nevertheless, the book was never full by the end of their school career. It would have been quite easy to have used half of this exercise book as a mathematical record, recording everything the children did, including results of any tests, and anything they had difficulty with. The children themselves could be involved in the recording as they were involved with their reading records.

Unfortunately, this idea did not occur to me at the time. A lot of good ideas come too late!

Discussion item 5

See Fig 10.4 (Turnbull, 1981, 1987).

Figure 10.4 This is part of a record sheet for pupils aged 9 to 12+ years. It is suggested that the following code is used:
✓ topic mastered
O topic partially learned
✗ topic not learned at all

CLASS .... Date	MONEY										PLACE VALUE										
	Concept of exchange, etc.	Coin recognition to 10p. Counting money to 20p. Equivalent amounts.	Shopping to 20p. Change.	50p coin and £1 note. Counting money to £1. Equivalent amounts.	Shopping to £1.	Decimal notation of the pound.	Shopping over £1.	Unit pricing. Best buys.	Simple money management. Discounts and increases in price.	Foreign currency.	Grouping experiences Number bases with two digits	Place value to 100.	Number bases with more than two digits. Alternative number systems	Place value to 1,000.	Tenths as decimals.	Hundredths as decimals.	Thousands, millions, etc.	Third and further decimal places.	One-to one correspondence.	Oral counting 0 - 10. Numerals 0 - 9.	
NAME	M 1	2	3	4	5	6	7	8	9	10	PV 1	2	3	4	5	6	7	8	N 1	2/3	4

Discussion item 6

See Fig 10.5 (ILEA, 1980).

Figure 10.5   This is part of one of four alternative forms of record sheet designed to be used with the ILEA *Checkpoints* Assessment Cards (ILEA Learning Materials, 1980). It is intended to provide a cummulative picture of a child's mathematical progress.

ALTERNATIVE 3

Name _____   School _____   from _____   to _____

Date of birth _____

Checkpoints assessment cards

Mathematics record

Stage A

Sets _____ date

Free sorting   Can choose a way to sort objects and explain what has been done   _____

Complementary sets   Can sort any objects into exactly two sets and explain the sorting using 'is' and 'is not'   _____

Re-sorting   Can choose a way to sort objects and can then choose a different way to sort them   _____

Numbers

Whole numbers

One-to-one correspondence   Can pair off the members of two sets to show whether there is a one-to-one correspondence between the two sets or not   _____

Conservation   Understands that the number of objects in a set is not changed by rearranging them   _____

Ordering   Can put sets in order according to the number of objects   _____

Numbers 0-9   Can make and count any set of up to nine objects. Can read, write and put in order the numerals 0-9   _____

Measures _____ date

Length

Conservation   Knows that when a line is bent or moved its length stays the same   _____

Ordering   Can put several objects in order of length and explain the relationships   _____

Time

Sequence and passing of time   Can talk about past, present and future events and time intervals and can put everyday events into sensible time sequences   _____

Cost

Simple shopping   Can pay up to 9p using 1p coins in shopping activities   _____

Capacity and volume

Conservation of volume   Knows that when the shape of a liquid or other substance is changed then the volume remains the same   _____

Direct comparison (capacity)   Can compare the capacities of two containers by pouring liquid from one to the other   _____

Weight

Conservation   Knows that if an object is deformed it is ... heavy ...

Discussion item 7: recording handout

What do we record?

1. Everything the child does.
2. Selections of things the child does.
3. Everything the child understands. Based upon:

   (a) Tests of some kind.

(b) Continuous observation of the child understanding this point.

(c) A single observation of the child understanding this point.

4. Selections of things the child understands. Based upon: (a), (b) and (c) above.

How do we record?

1. Checklists.
2. Boxes.
3. Written records.
4. Child's own work/child's own records.

Do we have any person/body we have to satisfy with our records? If so are any of the previous decisions taken from us? Do we particularly like anybody else's system, or do we need to design our own recording sheets/books/cards?

11
EVALUATION

Introduction

It is hoped that many of the chapters in this book have raised questions for you and your staff regarding the teaching and learning of mathematics in your school. Thinking about the implications of some of these questions and relating them to your own school may already have influenced the way you see your role as the co-ordinator for mathematics. This is the beginning of the evaluation process. It is the intention of this chapter to try to explain how an understanding of the processes of evaluation can help you to identify the concerns and influences which are at work in your school and to assist you in using these processes in a meaningful way.

At an early stage in this chapter it is necessary to make a clear distinction between evaluation, which is discussed here, and assessment which was introduced in the preceding chapter. However, it should be noted that many authors and, in particular those in the United States, suggest that there is very little difference between the two. In simplistic terms, we assess pupils to see what they have learnt, but use the term evaluation when considering the education being offered: that is, the suitability of the curriculum and the appropriateness and effectiveness of the teaching.

Evaluation is a very necessary part of the process of curriculum development, and curriculum development in mathematics is no exception to this. Without evaluation it is impossible to make any justifiable statements regarding the present situation of mathematics education in the school and therefore extremely difficult to direct any future planning. The Cockcroft Report (1982) commented on the fact that it believed that evaluation was not always carried out on a sufficient scale nor on a regular enough basis. The report added, 'it is only as a result of such evaluation that it is possible both to identify successful practice and also to identify areas in which help is required' (paragraph 424).

What is evaluation?

In the context of what has gone before in this book, evaluation needs to be seen as the process by which we come to terms with what is actually happening within a school in mathematics education. The process of evaluation should be viewed as a collaborative involvement exercise. All members of staff should participate in the activities and your role as the co-ordinator should be one of initiator. By working in this way opportunities are provided for raising issues in a non-threatening way, and the discussion that arises may well help to identify some of the in-service training needs of the staff. Key concepts in evaluation involve asking the right question at the right time and analysing the responses so as to be able to make informed judgements. Patton (1980) agrees with this definiton when he says that evaluation 'involves making judgements about and assigning value to what has been analysed and interpreted'.

We can see how Easen (1985) uses such a definition as this, in his model of the process of curriculum change (Fig. 11.1).

Figure 11.1   Box 3 shows the position of evaluation in the cycle

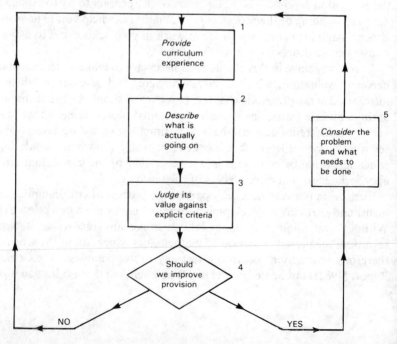

This may appear to be a fairly simplistic approach to the process of evaluation. However, there are many models of curriculum evaluation, but it is beyond the scope of this book to engage in any full-scale discussion of these. If the reader wishes to investigate further and develop his/her own knowledge, please consult the suggested reading section at the end of this chapter (page 167).

How to evaluate

Evaluation should be seen as a means by which the staff of a school are able to identify and prioritize necessary areas of concern or interest, and can subsequently work together towards developing their thinking. This should result in offering a more coherent, relevant, meaningful experience for the children in their care. As stated earlier evaluation must be a shared activity. It is best considered in terms of a shared model, of which the following is an example. This evaluation model involves the use of a five-stage process:

1. What is the purpose of the evaluation?
2. On which aspects of the mathematics curriculum do I wish to focus?
3. How do I obtain the information needed?
4. How do I make sense of the data collected?
5. What course of action do I take, if any?

Each of the five stages will now be considered in more detail. To aid the discussion a hypothetical example will be used drawn from a typical school experience: the headteacher has been requested by the governing body to provide an evaluation of the time devoted to mathematics by the school.

The purpose of the evaluation

The focus of the evaluation will depend largely on the reasons for it being undertaken. In the above example the purpose is to respond to the request from the governing body. The purpose behind their request is not directly known.

Aspects of the mathematics curriculum

You may feel that there are many aspects of mathematics education in your school which would benefit from careful consideration. However, it is essential that a carefully defined area is chosen, for example, focusing on the quality of classroom discussion. Too wide an area may well necessitate a consideration of too many variables and will result in difficulties in later analysis, thus making the evaluation ineffective. It may well be necessary to repeat the process several times before a clear overall picture is obtained. In the example above the aspect for consideration is already determined, namely how the school utilizes the time given to mathematics.

Obtaining the required information

Having decided whom the information is for and what is to be evaluated, there is now a need to consider what data is required and the best way of setting about collecting it. Because of the multiplicity of chosen situations, it is impossible to begin to list all the ways of obtaining such data.

The following are offered as likely ways of obtaining information:

1. working alongside other teachers;
2. talking with and working alongside children;
3. group and whole staff discussions;
4. observing teachers working with children;
5. analysing children's work;
6. keeping accurate records of what is happening in the classroom;
7. looking at testing and assessment procedures and subsequent results;
8. relating to your own experience;
9. discussions with parents.

It is hoped that the ways given will help you to see possible starting points to future evaluations.

The information needed for our example would appear to be best collected by each teacher keeping a written record of the amount of time spent by their own class on mathematics over a given period of, say, two weeks, using the following categories:

1. time spent on mathematics as an isolated subject;
2. time spent on mathematics in an integrated curricular approach;
3. time spent on incidental mathematics.

Alternatively, the headteacher could check individual timetables if these are available, although this would only give a global amount of time and it would not be possible to break it down further.

Making sense of the data

The first step will usually involve choosing a means of classifying the information obtained in order to assist the later analysis. In the example given it would be possible to classify into year groups, individual classes, infant and junior groups or by the three categories of where mathematics is found. The second step concerns the representation of the classified information and the communication of this information in an acceptable and meaningful form. Again this will largely depend on the intended audience.

The course of action

As a result of the analysis and the presentation of the findings, a decision may need to be taken about what action, if any, is necessary. Although originally the information was gathered as a direct result of a request from the governing body, the staff of the school may well wish to modify their teaching in the light of the results. In the example discussed this could involve:

1. a rethink of timetables;
2. a move towards a more integrated approach to mathematics;
3. a whole school discussion on the teaching of mathematics.

Often an evaluation of one particular aspect leads to further evaluation of one or more aspects. It must be remembered that the example above is based on a very simplistic model. Evaluations can be very involved and complicated. Self-evaluation can also have a built-in bias and steps to counteract this should be taken whenever possible. One common way is to involve outside agencies, although the staff of a school will often feel more threatened by evaluation of this kind. This is a point to guard against but is often unavoidable if a sense of reliability is desired.

Any evaluation of the mathematics education within your school would need to address the issues which form the basis of the individual chapters of this book. These can be classified under the following headings:

1. the needs of the children;
2. the aims and objectives of the school;
3. the effectiveness of the teaching.

In addition, it is necessary to consider the learning that has taken place by looking at the assessment of the children. This was discussed in detail in Chapter 10.

An evaluation in terms of these headings would provide information about the teaching and learning of mathematics that is taking place in the school but will not necessarily provide information that can inform you about the effectiveness of you in your role as co-ordinator. This part of the evaluation process will be discussed in the final part of the chapter.

Each of these will be considered as a separate entity, although it must be stressed that many of these aspects are interlinked with each other.

Evaluating the needs of the children

Every school should have an established philosophy of education, one part of which includes beliefs about the mathematical needs of the child and how these should integrate with the education of the whole child. Each school is required to have its own curriculum document for mathematics education, in which concerns relating to children's needs will be addressed. Because of the changing nature of these needs they should be examined and monitored on a regular basis. This examination and monitoring is part of the evaluation process.

In the process of evaluating the needs of the children, it would be advisable for the co-ordinator to reread the discussion in Chapter 4 which focuses on them in order to provide a means of examining the existing school policy. The school policy document is likely to have been drawn up using such documents as *Mathematics from 5 to 16* (DES, 1987), *Mathematics Counts* (Cockcroft, 1982) and various publications from the National Curriculum Council as a guide.

Within the broad area of children's needs there are many likely areas that may need to be evaluated. The following list is given as a guide and by no means is it exhaustive.

1. the attitude of girls to mathematics;
2. underachieving pupils;
3. poor self-image amongst pupils;
4. limiting recording methods;
5. poor communication skills;
6. inappropriate practical work;
7. lack of confidence in their own ability;
8. lack of enjoying mathematics.

Evaluating the aims and objectives of the school

Having established the needs of the children in mathematics, the staff will, at some time, have drawn up a comprehensive list of these aims and objectives that address these needs. Ideally these will have been drawn up by the whole staff and will reflect the overall aims and objectives for the school. Again, it would be useful to read again the relevant sections of Chapters 4 and 5. It is worth noting that the list should include aims and objectives in the affective domain as well as the cognitive domain, for example building up confidence in or developing the correct attitude to mathematics.

Although this chapter comes at the conclusion of the book, it is essential that evaluation is constantly taking place and indeed must begin as soon as the co-ordinator and staff are involved in any curriculum planning. If you are new to your post the first step is to consider the existing aims and objectives of the school. It would be a fruitless task, and very undesirable, if you began to change the aims and objectives without first evaluating the existing list (see Chapter 3). Remember this must be seen to be a collaborative exercise.

Once again there are several ways of achieving this. The one considered below involves the staff completing proformas on which they are asked a series of questions.

Step one: issuing the proformas

Write in the space below what you consider *are* the aims and objectives for mathematics in our school.

Now list what you consider the aims and objectives *should be.*

You will need to wait a few days for the return of the proformas, but in the meantime you will be drawing up your own list.

Step two

Read all the comments from the staff about what they consider the aims and objectives to be. (Do not be surprised if you find there are many discrepancies among the comments of the staff, as aims and objectives are a grey area in schools.)

Step three

Now it is down to your own judgement. To what extent do these aims match with the school aims and objectives stated in the school's policy document on mathematics? If there are widespread discrepancies you are faced with a problem. You have two choices:

1. If you consider the school's aims and objectives to be appropriate, then you must make other members of staff aware of what they are according to the curriculum document.
2. If the school's aims and objectives are not seen as appropriate they should be amended accordingly in line with yours and the other teachers' lists.

It is important when you make decisions like the one above to consider very carefully the grounds on which you and the staff make them. It is quite common to receive comments like, 'I know what is right for my children' or 'I've been teaching for 20 years'. It would be wrong to argue that experience does not give one a good insight into what is right and wrong in a particular school. However, it is so easy to become so involved that you 'cannot see the wood for the trees'. More importantly, though, it is essential that you as the mathematics co-ordinator can back up claims and statements with strong evidence. As stated earlier, the collection of evidence is a key element in the evaluation process, and it is very important that you read as widely as possible making brief notes on any key facts that you may come across. For example, the results of the APU attitude survey would be useful when trying to justify a change of direction in the mathematics education of girls.

Step four

The decision should be communicated to all the staff and any necessary amendments made to the school's curriculum document.

The effectiveness of the teaching

It is so easy for teachers and others to look at the performance of the children and to blame the children themselves for the lack of success. Although this could be the case, it is often necessary to look more closely at the situation and in particular at the teaching methods employed. Even the best teachers will fail if they are using inappropriate methods. But how does a school consider the teaching it employs and, having analysed subsequent results, make the necessary changes? This is the third consideration of the evaluation process that will be discussed. Teachers find themselves becoming more and more accountable to a variety of groups of people. These include the headteacher, the governors, LEA advisers and inspectors, parents and, in the immediate future, the attainment targets and assessment of the National Curriculum. Accountability and evaluation are so interwoven when considering the teaching found in a school that often the two are indistinguishable. It must be added, however, that while accountability presupposes evaluation, evaluation does not necessarily imply accountability. The critical appraisal of teachers which has recently come to the fore will hopefully include evaluation as a major element.

How then can a teacher, or groups of teachers (as it must be remembered that evaluation is a collaborative process) improve their performance? First, and perhaps most importantly, they must realize and accept that the fault for a child not learning some key aspect may be the result of their own teaching. House (1972) suggests that a teacher may not have much to gain but very much more to lose from evaluation of their teaching:

> After all, what does a teacher have to gain from having his work examined? As he sees it, absolutely nothing. He is exposing himself to administrators and parents. He risks damage to his ego by finding out he is not doing his job as well as he thinks. Perhaps worst of all, he risks discovering that his students do not really care for him, something a teacher would rather not know. The culture of the school offers no rewards for examining one's behavior – only penalties. Since there are no punishments for not exposing one's behavior and many dangers in so doing, the prudent teacher gives lip service to the idea and drags both feet.

This quotation may be exaggerating the problem, but there is a great amount of truth in it, and teachers must have confidence that the evaluations will help them improve their teaching. They also must come to value self-evaluation.

Collecting information to enable a teacher to self-evaluate needs careful consideration. Any attempt to try to do too much at once will probably lead to failure. Select something small and manageable. For example, if a teacher wishes to evaluate the type of questioning they use in discussion with their class, it would be very difficult to remember the questions asked at the end of a session. Better to use a tape-recording which can be transcribed and analysed when time permits. There are several advantages and disadvantages to using tape-recorders. The advantages include: they allow the collection of ample material for later analysis; they can be used to demonstrate the teacher's development in various techniques. The disadvantages include the fact that the children may be distracted by the equipment and the lack of recording any non-verbal communication.

The example of questioning detailed above is only one of many possible areas that could be evaluated. Cockcroft (1982, paragraph 243) outlines six aspects of teaching mathematics that could usefully be used as a basis for evaluation. Many books are available on teaching styles and the role of the teacher, and readers interested in this area should find plenty to interest them.

It is very likely that other members of staff will show some reluctance to becoming involved in the evaluative process. However, the co-ordinator must use the results of their self-evaluation to encourage other teachers to use the same techniques in their classroom, if necessary purely for their own information. Pressure to publicize shortcomings or strengths will only produce a barrier which the co-ordinator will find very difficult to break down. In an ideal world staff would share their findings with their colleagues, and through the resulting discussion identify strengths and weaknesses requiring attention, perhaps through in-service education, particularly school-based if problems identified are common among several members of the staff.

Evaluating the effectiveness of the mathematics co-ordinator

Having considered ways of evaluating the needs of the children, the aims and objectives of the school, and the effectiveness of the children it is now time to examine the role of the co-ordinator. There are many ways of evaluating the role played by the mathematics co-ordinator and many aspects to consider. Chapter 1 discusses the role of the co-ordinator, and one way to evaluate would be to consider some of the items in the job specifications given in the various publications. For convenience, another list of possible roles is given on page 165–166. Another way of looking at the role of the co-ordinator is to evaluate their personal qualities. Figure 11.2 illustrates an advert that appeared as part of an in-service training (INSET) course.

It would seem that an evaluation of these points – that is, the ability to administrate, instigate, activate, co-ordinate, demonstrate and stimulate, together with the lack of pontification – would provide a very clear picture of how the co-ordinator is operating. As stated earlier, an evaluation could be done by someone known to the co-ordinator. In this case the evaluater could be the headteacher, an adviser or advisory teacher, or a teaching colleague who was experienced in evaluation. Alternatively a more independent evaluation by an outside agency could be sought, for example a mathematics education lecturer from a neighbouring higher education institution. Although self-evaluation would be possible, it is not recommended in this case if the results are to be viewed with some degree of acceptance.

Figure 11.2

The possible methods of evaluation are not dissimilar to those discussed earlier. However, it must be remembered that any data collected reflect the personal nature of a professional and great care must be exercised at all times if embarrassment is to be avoided. This situation particularly applies when questioning other members of staff about the co-ordinator. It must not be seen as 'trial without a jury'. The results of any evaluation must be used to develop the effectiveness of the co-ordinator and must not be used to judge whether the person in question is worth any extra allowance. Such misuse of data is fraught with problems.

If evaluation of personal qualities is not seen as being useful, consideration of the list below of possible responsibilities would help to develop a 'profile' of the effectiveness of the co-ordinator. The list is not exhaustive and is for illustration only.

1. decisions regarding the ordering of books and equipment;
2. assessing the state of mathematics in the school;

3. running in-service training (INSET) for the rest of the staff;
4. keeping abreast of current thinking in the subject;
5. advising the headteacher on colleagues' strengths and weaknesses;
6. organizing schemes of work for colleagues;
7. keeping parents in touch with what is happening in mathematics;
8. storage and distribution of mathematics materials;
9. devising special programmes to cater for special needs.

It is not possible to overemphasize the importance of evaluation. Generally speaking it is a neglected area that needs to be considered as soon as any curriculum development begins to take place or when someone takes on a new role. Assessment of children is only a small part of the evaluative process, but perhaps it is the part which receives the most attention. Good teachers are constantly evaluating the mathematics education they are giving their children. Similarly, a good co-ordinator is forever questioning his/her own effectiveness to the rest of the staff and school in general.

Summary

Throughout this book the importance of assessment and evaluation has been stressed. As co-ordinator one of the most difficult tasks you must undertake is to evaluate the effectiveness of the mathematics programme in your school. Some of the fundamental questions you should ask when first looking at your school are discussed in Chapter 3. In this chapter attention has been focused on the main areas that you will need to consider as you and your colleagues become involved in the ongoing process of evaluation.

Evaluation should be seen as a collaborative exercise and should focus on:

1. the needs of children;
2. the aims and objectives of the school's mathematics programme;
3. the effectiveness of the teaching.

It is important that you consider your own performance in the role of co-ordinator. This will involve some self-evaluation but it also requires a constructive and sensitive appraisal by others.

References

Cockcroft, W.H. (Chairman) (1982) *Mathematics Counts* (Report of the Committee of Inquiry), HMSO, London.
DES (1987) *Mathematics from 5 to 16: Curriculum Matters 3*, 2nd Edition, HMSO, London.

Easen, P. (1985) *Making School-Centred INSET Work*, Open University/Croom Helm, Milton-Keynes/London.

House, E.R. (1973) The conscience of educational evaluation, in House, E.R. (ed) *School Education: The Politics and Process*, McCutchan Publishing Corp., Berkeley, California.

Patton, M.Q. (1980) *Qualitative Evaluation Methods*, Sage Publications, Beverly Hills, California.

Recommended reading

Anderson, D.C. (1981) *Evaluating Curriculum Proposals*, Croom Helm, London.

Blenkin, G.M. and Kelly, A.V. (1981) *The Primary Curriculum*, Paul Chapman Publishing, London.

Blenkin, G.M. and Kelly, A.V. (1983) *The Primary Curriculum in Action*, Paul Chapman Publishing, London.

Davis, E. (1981) *Teachers as Curriculum Evaluators*, Allen and Unwin, London.

McCormick, R. and James, M. (1983) *Curriculum Evaluation in Schools*, Croom Helm, London.

Schools Council (1973) *Evaluation in Curriculum Development*, Macmillan, London.

Schools Council (1976) *Curriculum Evaluation Today: Trends and implications*, Macmillan, London.

Wiseman, S. (1970) *Curriculum Evaluation*, NFER, London.

APPENDIX

A group of teachers, when asked how they would evaluate the teaching of mathematics in a school, devised the following list of questions:

The curriculum

1. Have the aims of mathematics teaching been discussed and agreed by the teachers?
2. Is a list of some aims included in the teaching syllabus?
3. Is it clear from the teaching syllabus what knowledge, skills and abilities are to be developed with each age group and ability level?
4. Are teachers given guidance on how the teaching syllabus can be classified into learning objectives for the pupils?
5. Do the aims include some relating to attitudes towards mathematics as well as to the acquisition of mathematical knowledge?
6. Do the aims consider the backgrounds (for example, home situation, language difficulties) of the pupils in the school?
7. Has the previous kind of mathematical experience of the pupils been taken into consideration?
8. Is there cohesion and continuity in the development of the mathematics curriculum?

The teaching

1. Is there a clear rationale for the ways in which teaching groups are organized?
2. Is sufficient individual work planned for each year group?
3. Are there attempts to identify which topics are best taught to individuals, to groups, to a whole class?
4. Does each teacher vary his/her teaching style to meet the needs of the occasion?
5. Are pupils encouraged to develop their own ways of learning?
6. Do the teachers make specific efforts to develop the pupils' interest in mathematics?
7. Are efforts made to ensure the pupils are well motivated to learn?
8. Is the material made relevant and the work purposeful in mathematics?
9. Is the right balance given to the memorization of facts, the mastery of rules and the understanding of concepts?
10. Is there the opportunity for children to discuss, talk and write about some of the mathematics they have learned (or are learning)?
11. Is there adequate provision for the needs of pupils with specific learning problems, for underachievers, for slow-learners, for very-able pupils?
12. Are there means available for teachers to evaluate the pupils' attainments, to diagnose pupils' learning difficulties and to assess the effectiveness of their own teaching?

Resources

1. Is there an adequate supply of textbooks, workcards, materials, equipment and visual aids?
2. Are duplicating and reprographic facilities available?
3. Are staff aware of the resources available?
4. Can staff gain access to resources readily?
5. Is the accommodation (classrooms and furniture) appropriate to the teaching methods used?
6. Are displays in the classrooms aesthetically pleasing and likely to stimulate learning?

Staff

1. Do teachers have the opportunity to be involved in planning the mathematics programme of the school?
2. Do the teachers co-operate and share ideas and resources?
3. Are there opportunities for the teachers to meet formally to discuss all aspects of teaching mathematics in the school?
4. Are the teachers encouraged to attend conferences and courses outside school to develop their professional skills in teaching mathematics?
5. Is there available in the school a collection of reference material and periodicals to provide a stimulus and source of new ideas?
6. Is there a teacher with responsibility for the co-ordination of mathematics in the school?
7. Do teachers have the opportunity to see each other in action?

12
BRINGING ABOUT CHANGE

The implementation of the National Curriculum is bound to be a major task for all primary schools in the next few years. However, it would be both unwise and incorrect to assume that having prescribed attainment targets and programmes of study will somehow, by themselves, raise the standards of mathematics teaching in your school. The attainment targets and the programmes of study define a syllabus in the narrow sense and not a curriculum in the wide sense. You, in consultation with your colleagues, will still need to decide the teaching approaches, the classroom organization, the types of activities and experiences, and the use of resources.

You may find the following points helpful when thinking about these wider issues.

Teaching approaches

Consider the importance of:

1. the *do–talk–record* model of mathematics teaching;
2. providing opportunities for pupils to discuss mathematics amongst themselves and with the teacher;
3. practical work, mental arithmetic, problem-solving and investigational work;
4. ensuring that pupils develop, and become accurate and confident in using mathematical language.

Classroom organization
Think about the need for a mixture of:
1. individual work;
2. group activities;
3. whole class teaching.

Activities and experience

The National Curriculum Council offers the following guidance. The selection of activities chosen by a teacher for a particular group of pupils will vary from school to school, from class to class, and from pupil to pupil. The overall design and balance of any plan of work should, however, be based upon the following guidelines:

1. Activities should bring together different areas of mathematics,
2. The order of activities should be flexible,
3. Activities should be balanced between tasks that develop knowledge, skills and understanding and those that develop the ability to tackle practical problems,
4. Activities should be balanced between the applications of mathematics and ideas that are purely mathematical,
5. Activities should be balanced between those that are short in duration and those that have scope for development over an extended period,
6. Activities should, where appropriate, use pupils' own interests or questions either as starting points or as further lines of development,
7. Activities should, where appropriate, involve both independent and co-operative work,
8. Tasks should include those which have an exact result or answer and those which have many possible outcomes,
9. Activities should be balanced between different modes of learning: doing, observing, talking and listening, discussing with teachers and other pupils, reflecting, drafting, reading and writing,
10. Activities should encourage pupils to use mental arithmetic and pencil-and-paper methods, and to become confident in the use of a range of mathematical tools and new technology.
11. Activities should enable pupils to communicate their mathematics.
12. Activities should enable pupils to develop their personal qualities.
13. Activities should enable pupils to develop a positive attitude to mathematics.

Assessment

Assessment should:

1. be a continuous, ongoing process;

2. provide a means of diagnosing pupils' difficulties;
3. help a teacher to plan a programme of mathematics;
4. find out what children know as well as what they do not know.

Resources

Consider the need to provide resources for:

1. practical activities in mathematics;
2. cross-curricular activities (linking science and mathematics, for example);
3. calculator work;
4. using computers as an aid to learning mathematics and to provide suitable databases.

In Chapters 3 and 11 we raise the questions you might ask yourself about mathematics teaching in your school. Having thought about these questions you may feel dissatisfied with some aspects. How can you begin to tackle the task of bringing about changes?

There are several stages in the process.

Stage 1   Identify the needs in relation to both the pupils and the teachers. Which needs are not being met?

Stage 2   Analyse the problem by breaking it down into manageable parts. The analysis will require reflection on present practice and a sharing of experiences.

Stage 3   Develop a plan. Decide what you can build upon. It will require free and frank discussions with colleagues in order to reach a consensus on what actions to take.

Stage 4   Work together to bring about change. Views and experiences have to be shared.

Stage 5   Evaluate how successful you, as a group, have been in bringing about change. Collect evidence from classroom observations, by talking to pupils, by analysing results in assessment tasks or by whatever other means are appropriate to the situation.

Bringing about change is a continuous process. Having reached stage 5 you will probably want to go back to stage 1 to begin tackling a different problem! Bringing about change is also a collaborative exercise. It will only be successful if *everyone* is involved. Then the change can be seen as *our* change and not something imposed from outside. That way it will have more of a long-term effect!

11
ANNOTATED BIBLIOGRAPHY

The following list contains books that are likely to be of particular value and interest to a primary mathematics co-ordinator. The references at the end of each chapter provide a valuable additional source of further reading.

Reports

Cockcroft, W.H. (Chairman) (1982) *Mathematics Counts* (Report of the Committee of Inquiry), HMSO, London.
Still the definitive document about mathematics teaching.
DES (1979) *Mathematics 5–11: A Handbook of Suggestions*, HMSO, London.
Contains suggestions on the teaching of specific topics as well as the planning of a mathematics programme.
DES (1989) *Mathematics in the National Curriculum*, DES and Welsh Office, London.
Contains all the details of attainment targets and programmes of study.
HMI (1989) *Aspects of Primary Education: The Teaching and Learning of Mathematics*, HMSO, London.

The role of the mathematics co-ordinator

ATM (1987) *Co-ordinating Mathematics in Primary and Middle Schools*, Association of Teachers of Mathematics, Derby.
A discussion document containing many activities suitable for in-service training (INSET) exercises.
Stow, M. with Foxman, D. (1988) *Mathematics Coordination*, NFER-Nelson, Windsor.
The report of a research project studying the role of the mathematics co-ordinator.

Choosing a published textbook scheme

Harling, P. and Roberts, T. (1988) *Primary Mathematics Schemes*, Hodder and Stoughton, Sevenoaks.
Includes a list of criteria for assessing the suitability of a scheme as well as comments on various schemes.

Mathematical Association (1986) *Choosing a Primary School Mathematics Textbook or Scheme*, The Mathematical Association, Leicester.
A folder containing six papers to be worked through by teachers as a means of helping them to choose a scheme.

Turnbull, J. (1981/87) *Maths Links 1 and 2*, NARE Publications, Stafford.
Contains cross-references to most published schemes arranged under topics. Associated tests and record-sheets available. Volume 1 refers to earlier books and schemes.

Current issues

Association of Science Education (1989) *The National Curriculum – Making it Work for the Primary School*, ASE, Hatfield.
Produced jointly with the Association of Teachers of Mathematics, the Mathematical Association and the National Association for the Teaching of English. It looks at a cross-curricular approach to work in the infant school.

Hughes, M. (1986) *Children and Number*, Basil Blackwell, Oxford.
Looks at the difficulties young children have with basic number concepts and suggests new approaches.

Lumb, D. (1987) *Teaching Mathematics 5 to 11*, Croom Helm, London.
A survey of the current state of mathematics teaching, including children's learning difficulties, investigations and problem-solving, calculators and computers.

Preston, M. (ed) (1987) *Mathematics in Primary Education*, Falmer Press, Lewes.
A multi-author book that considers key issues in mathematics education.

Shuard, H. (1986) *Primary Mathematics Today and Tomorrow*, Longman for SCDC, York.
A wide-ranging survey resulting from the feasibility study for what became the PrIME project.

Teaching primary mathematics

Biggs, E. and Sutton, J. (1983) *Teaching Mathematics 5 to 9*, McGraw-Hill, Maidenhead.

Deboys, M. and Pitt, E. (1980 2nd edn.), *Lines of Development in Primary Mathematics*, Blackstaff Press, Belfast.

Merrtens, R. (1987) *Teaching Primary Mathematics*, Edward Arnold, London.

Paling, D. (1982) *Teaching Mathematics in Primary Schools*, Oxford University Press, Oxford.

Williams, E.M. and Shuard, H.B. (1982) *Primary Mathematics Today*, 3rd edition, Longman, London.
All the above cover the main topics in the primary mathematics curriculum and give suggestions on their development and suitable activities.

Investigations and problem-solving

Burton, L. (1986) *Thinking Things Through*, Basil Blackwell, Oxford.
An analysis of the problem-solving process in mathematics, with many examples.
Mottershead, L. (1977) *Sources of Mathematical Discovery*, Basil Blackwell, Oxford.
Provides the starting point for many activities and projects, which can be tackled at many different levels.
Several of the textbook schemes produce supplementary material on investigations, notably Peak Maths *Peak Plus* (Nelson), Nuffield Maths *Challengers* (Longman) and Ginn Maths *Investigations, Games and Puzzles* (Ginn). In addition, many associations and institutions produce booklets of materials. Send for lists to NORMAC publications, Tarquin, Eigen publications, Mathematical Association, Association of Teachers of Mathematics and Manchester Polytechnic (Gillian Hatch). Addresses are given on page 177-178.

Language in mathematics

Brissenden, T. (1988) *Talking About Mathematics*, Basil Blackwell, Oxford.
The importance of mathematical discussion in primary classrooms and ways of encouraging it.
Mathematical Association (1987) *Maths Talk*, The Mathematical Association/Stanley Thorne, Leicester/Cheltenham.
Language in primary mathematics - listening, talking and developing skills.
Shuard, H. and Rothery, A. (eds) (1984) *Children Reading Mathematics*, John Murray, London.
A comprehensive study of factors affecting readability in mathematics. Takes examples from a wide range of sources but includes a number at primary level.

Multicultural issues

ILEA (1986) *Everyone Counts: Looking for Bias and Insensitivity in Primary Mathematic Materials*, Inner London Education Authority, Learning Resources Branch, London.
Looks for bias and insensitivity in primary maths material.
Mathematical Association (1988) *Mathematics in a Multicultural Society*, The Mathematical Association, Leicester.
A collection of articles looking at different aspects.

Girls and mathematics

Burton, L. (ed) (1986) *Girls into Maths Can Go*, Holt, Rinehart and Winston, London.
A wide-ranging collection of articles covering all the main issues.

Low-attaining pupils

Denvir, B., Stolz, C. and Brown, M. (1982) *Low Attainers in Mathematics 5-16: Policies and Practices in School*, Methuen Educational, London.
Report of a Schools Council Project looking at policies and practices; contains examples of classroom work.
Dickson, L., Brown, M. and Gibson, O. (1984) *Children Learning Mathematics*, Holt, Rinehart and Winston, London.
A survey of research in the field written for teachers. Considers spatial thinking, measurement, number and language.

Computers

Ainley, J. and Goldstein, R. (1988) *Making LOGO Work*, Basil Blackwell, Oxford.
Shows use of LOGO in school classrooms, both primary and secondary. Includes chapters on using a floor turtle and on how LOGO can help children learn mathematics.
Ball, D. (1986) *Microcomputers in Mathematics Teaching*, Hutchinson Educational, London.
Considers all the general issues.
Papert, S. (1980) *Mindstorms: Children, Computers and Powerful Ideas*, Harvester Press, Brighton.
The book that first made educationalists think about how computers could help children to learn.

Calculators

ATM/MA (1986) *Calculators in the Primary School*, Association of Teachers of Mathematics/Mathematical Association, Derby/Leicester.
A collection of articles from *Mathematics Teaching* and *Mathematics in School*.
Open University (1982) *Calculators in the Primary School*, The Open University, Milton Keynes.
The role of the calculator in relation to the primary mathematics curriculum; the calculator as a means of learning skills and concepts and of aiding problem-solving.
Details of the CAN (Calculator-aware Number Curriculum) can be obtained from the PrIME project.

Curriculum development

Easen, P. (1985) *Making School-Centred INSET Work*, Open University/Croom Helm, Milton Keynes/London.
How to negotiate curriculum change.

USEFUL ADDRESSES

Association of Teachers of
    Mathematics,
Kings Chambers,
Queen Street,
Derby, DE1 3DA

Eigen Publications,
39 Den Bank Crescent,
Sheffield, S10 5PB

Gillian Hatch,
Manchester Polytechnic,
Didsbury School of Education,
779 Wilmslow Road,
Manchester, M20 8RR

ILEA (Inner London Education
    Authority)
Learning Resources Branch,
275 Kennington Lane,
London, SE11 5QZ

The Mathematical Association,
259 London Road,
Leicester, LE2 3BE

NORMAC,
Education Development Service,
c/o Margaret Ashton Lower School,
Monsall Road,
Manchester, M10 8WP

PrIME Project,
Homerton College,
Cambridge, CB2 2PH

Tarquin Publications,
Stradbroke,
Diss
Norfolk, IP21 5JP

INDEX